GRAVELED
WAYS

John H. Odden

Bozeman, MT

11/10/13

GRAVELED WAYS

A memoir

JOHN McILVAIN

For the next generation

Library of Congress Cataloging-in-Publication Data available upon request.

ISBN-13: 978-1492144861
ISBN-10: 149214486X

Made in America
Designed by Suzanne LaGasa
Typeset in Adobe Caslon

The photograph on page is 136 printed with permission from the Keewaydin Foundation. All other photographs and illustrations are from the collection of John McIlvain.

10 9 8 7 6 5 4 3 2 1

TABLE OF CONTENTS

Graveled Ways

O what if levelled lawns and gravelled ways...
But take our greatness with our violence?

W.B. Yeats
MEDITATION IN A TIME OF CIVIL WAR

PREFACE

I first sat down to write this memoir thirty-five years ago when I was half my current age. I wanted to write about my boyhood and adolescence before time eroded my memory of them. Under the influence of Lillian Hellman's *Pentimento*, I had literary aspirations. Unfortunately my youth lacked both the drama of her life and the expansiveness of the stage she performed on. The manuscript rested in a drawer until recently when Wendy McIlvain, a member of my family's next generation, expressed curiosity about how mine grew up. I regretted not knowing (or asking) more about my grandmother's and my parents' childhoods and decided to revisit this version of my youth and share what came of it.

What I found I had written was narrowly focused on some selected experiences that I thought had shaped me. In this revision I have tried to work in details that I originally took for granted, but now seem worth noting because they give a sense of a world that has gone. I have found myself wishing I had been more of a journalist and less self-absorbed when I embarked on this project. The person who wrote at that time is as different from me now as he thought he was from the person he was writing about. I have tried to produce a sharper picture and one that I feel less self-conscious about having friends and family read.

The times when I grew up were very different from today's. Televisions were small screens in large cabinets, there was no global village, and what I knew about the world beyond my immediate circle was stitched together from snippets of information and rumor. Teenage excesses were limited mainly to alcohol and tobacco. I became curious about what I was not (Catholic, Jewish, Negro, female) gradually and was disabused of my ignorance slowly.

I led what many would call a sheltered, privileged life, one without brutality or hardship. Everything was restrained. More often than not, I think of myself as enjoying a happy childhood. This strikes me as almost entirely rooted in the world my brothers David and Eddie occupied, filled with imaginary exploits and fantasies of heroism. I have been surprised by my apparent isolation and the depth of my tendency to mimic my peers, but relieved that I discovered ways of enjoying the energy of life and of those who shared it.

December, 2012

FOREBEARS

At the end of a wintery spring in 1917, my mother, Peggy Seyburn, began her long life on a beautiful June day in a vibrant and bustling Detroit. Her mother, Winifred Dodge—known as Seebee to me and my generation, Winnie to her friends—was the eldest daughter of John Francis Dodge, one of two inseparable brothers who were busy living the rags to riches American dream. They had earned their fortunes during the twenty years before my mother's birth because they were industrious and talented mechanics in the right place at the right time. Their first venture had been bicycles, then the transmissions for the Oldsmobile, then, risking all, the transmission and engine for the original Ford. Before building the first Dodge automobile in 1914, Dodge Brothers was the largest auto parts manufacturing company in America. At the time my mother was born, the brothers had retooled their factory to produce howitzers for the war effort they embraced. The Dodges loved to boast that the first Dodge had come to America in 1628. If so, they had squandered almost three hundred years in the New World before amounting to something.

A picture suggests John Dodge was aggressive, stubborn, and proud. His head appears to be bolted on, and stiff collar or not, able to turn like a tank's turret. Even inside his fine Edwardian suit, no gentleman resides. His considerable bulk is meat and potatoes, not puff pastry. He is clean-shaven and round faced, and his determined eyes, said to be blue and piercing, bulge.

He took pride in his vices. "I'd hate to think the world believes you have to drink sarsaparilla to get rich." Likely this was an allusion to Ford and Rockefeller, whose teetotaling sanctimony riled him. His money came too late, and he died too early, to accommodate pretension. He left it to his children and grandchildren to master the finger bowl. He earned enough billions, in today's money, so that even after being divided and spent, divided and spent, and divided again, what remains makes the lives of his great-grandchildren easier.

But he had little time to be a father. Seebee's childhood was not an easy one. Her mother, Ivy Hawkins, who was the source of the remarkable beauty Seebee and her daughters inherited, died of tuberculosis when Seebee was six. A heart wrenching letter that Ivy wrote Seebee at the time has vanished, but a similar one to Seebee's younger sister Isabel still exists.

854 Trumbull Avenue
Aug 21st, 1901

My dear curly headed baby girl,

Mama will try and write a letter to you to be read many years from now.

Mama is propped up with pillows to write this. She has been in bed most two weeks and feels awfully weak and shaky.

Mama feels so bad when she looks at her three darling babies to think of leaving them, but God's will be done. He will look after you all.

I hope you will be a good, honest, truthful girl, trusting in Jesus.

Oh darling, I want you both to be strong in resisting temptation.

Think of your mother. I want to be able to watch you and guide you aright.

Mama has divided her silver as she thinks it will be satisfactory to her darlings—knives, forks, tablespoons, teaspoons, berry spoons and various little things. You must not put the handles of knives and forks in water. They turn yellow.

Friday, August 23rd

You see, dearest, Mama was not able to finish your letter and she feels worse today and so will not write much.

I pray our Heavenly Father to look after my three little

darlings. May this blessing rest on you always.

Love your sister and brother. They are all you have in this world besides Papa.

Goodbye my darling.

Till we meet in Heaven.

From

Mother

Later, Isabel (left) and Winifred (right) endured a stepmother who put coal in their Christmas stocking and who their father never even acknowledged as his wife. (I believe John Dodge's sister-in-law Anna Dodge convinced him to marry her spinster friend Eleanor Smith so there would be someone to look after his three children.) When Seebee reached adolescence, John Dodge remarried a second time. This time his bride was his secretary. I suspect Seebee and Isabel were rarely parented, but they did have one another until Seebee married William Gray at twenty-one. During much of this time, their younger brother John Duval was on the periphery, relegated during adolescence to a series of schools that expelled him. Seebee and Isabel remained close for the rest of their lives, best friends as well as sisters, blessed in many ways. But their mother's prayers for their brother went unanswered. John Dodge, who died along with his brother from the flu in 1921, disinherited John Duval over a precipitous marriage, and though his sisters did what they could for him, his life was marked with failure. He died in his forties in police custody, apparently after being arrested for raucous behavior while trying to escape from a neighbor's houseguest's bedroom window.

Two years after Seebee married William, my mother Peggy was born; three years later, her sister, Suzanne. The family lived in Indian Village, which even today remains a relatively upscale section of Detroit. Their house was a large Tudor that continues to be one of the most impressive in the neighborhood, a wedding present from John Dodge. My mother remembered the home of her early childhood as one of long, dark corridors. She tended to shiver when anyone asked her about it.

Peggy never got to know her father. I did not even know of his existence until I read a legal document in Seebee's house in Detroit that detailed Peggy's adoption by Wesson Seyburn, the man I had always thought was my biological grandfather. Wesson had previously been married to Gwendolyn Currie, who came to be known to us years later as the Countess Tolstoy. The Seyburns (Wesson and the Countess) and the Grays (William and Seebee) had been neighbors. The night after I found out that I had an alternate grandfather in William Gray, Seebee invited the Countess for dinner. Their husbands had died; their hatchets were buried.

Seebee with pearls, perhaps an engagement picture (left). The Seyburn sisters Isabel, Suzanne, Peggy, and Edith on the steps of The Sycamores.

What William Gray had done to be erased from his family is unknown. He was a lawyer and a banker, the son of a banker who had married a woman of considerable prominence, Hannah Van Vechten, so his family was therefore more than respectable enough for the daughter of an upstart like John Dodge. In any case, William Gray vanished, seen only once more by Peggy at her paternal grandparents' house and never again by his other daughter Suzanne. We assume some money was involved. Some years ago, Suzanne's daughter Brooke, divorced and looking for a name, took his. Seebee would not have approved but could protest only from the grave. She had died on the third of January, 1980, on the day her father's plant, Dodge Main, turned out its last car.

Seebee and Wesson were the perfect twenties couple. Carefree and careless, they delegated the parenting of their four girls—Peggy and Suzanne, whom Wesson adopted, and Edith and Isabel, who were their natural children—to governesses, while they embraced the good life and dabbled in fast boats and racehorses. My mother, like her mother before her, latched onto the sister nearest to her. Their new home in Grosse Pointe, a faux French chateau dubbed The Sycamores, was grand but not exactly child friendly, its façade vaguely suggestive of an emperor's mausoleum.

When she was fifteen or so, my mother went away to Virginia, to Foxcroft School, where she felt exiled and did poorly in chemistry, but formed at least one lifelong friendship. After graduating, she spent a year in Florence at finishing school. Somewhere along the line she must have had an inspirational English teacher for I have first editions of Hemingway, Thomas Wolfe, *Light in August*, and *Absalom! Absalom!*, with "Peggy Seyburn" written in them. Her happiest time seems to have been a trip to Europe in 1936 with the Countess and Wesson's daughter Gwen. While there, the stepsisters went to Bayreuth, where Hitler appeared. This adventure was followed by a miniature grand tour of the continent, which included The Orient Express, Istanbul, and a successful swim across the Dardanelles. Peggy later developed a passion for photography and in the early years of my life was a photographer for the Red Cross—her war effort. She also took and developed endless shots of her oldest child, me.

I do not think it a coincidence that all of the Seyburn sisters fled Grosse Pointe. Three married Eastern prep school, Ivy League graduates, and one an Argentinean of great charm. None had any interest in coming home again. They had gone east: to Virginia for school, to Manchester in the summer, to Palm Beach in the winter. Away from home, each could be like a Jamesian heroine in Europe. Everything about Grosse Pointe must have seemed stultifying. The sisters must have felt they had little in common with their fellow midwesterners. I picture my mother, after her

year in Florence and the travels that followed, embracing her continental sophistication. She spoke Italian and French. Going home to Detroit was like returning to prison, albeit one with a Renoir and a Cezanne and very fine Louis XV furniture, from which she needed to escape.

Though I never felt trapped in its corridors and instead explored each room as a place touched with mystery and the promise of adventure, I can understand how my mother must have felt about The Sycamores. Seebee and Wesson moved into the house shortly after John Dodge's death. It was a place without warmth, especially as Seebee's two other houses were so different. Casa Giravento in Palm Beach, now a landmark, was more modest in its demeanor and as light-filled as the Grosse Pointe stronghold was dark. The downstairs of Casa Giravento opened to a fountained patio, which seemed an extension of the loggia that fronted it; walking into the house you found yourself in a tiled hall with plants that arched over your head as if the garden had followed you through the door. The windows were always open to soft winds or the music of the water in the fountains, and the scent of gardenias perfumed the air. In summer, there was Cobb Cottage, the house in Manchester-by-the-Sea, Massachusetts, which Seebee had bought so her daughters could blossom on the breezy shores of the Atlantic instead of along the breathless shores of Lake St. Clair. Cobb Cottage seemed the antithesis of The Sycamores. It was informal not austere, clapboard not stone, and a place where the laughter of children could sweep through the rooms instead of echoing in shadows.

All of the houses in which my mother had grown up were familiar to me, and so in their way provide a context for her childhood. The corridors and the rooms of the New York brownstone where my father, Eddie McIlvain, spent most of his childhood is buried somewhere under Rockefeller Center, and I have no idea of the location of the house he lived in during his earliest years in Pennsylvania, save that it was probably in Bethlehem where he was born in 1896—more than twenty years before my mother—on the Fourth of July like my grandson Angus. My brother David did go to the Hill School, the same boarding school our father had attended some forty-five years earlier, but all I have are mementos.

Eddie, far right, as the lead (Lt. Archibald Chomondeley) in *Fi, Fie, Foe, Fum,* a 1915 Princeton Triangle show.

After Hill, Eddie went to Princeton where he had the lead in a Triangle Club show that was written by Scott Fitzgerald. He left Princeton before graduating to attend the Naval War College, becoming a lieutenant and serving at the end of World War I on a destroyer. He held a number of different jobs in the twenties and thirties. One of the first was with J.P. Morgan, which placed him in Paris for a while; later he worked for the agent Leland Hayward. This might have been either just before or when he was courting my mother. I like to picture him author dropping or perhaps introducing her to Somerset Maugham, whom she would dazzle with her beauty and ask if he, too, read D.H. Lawrence.

The source of most of what I know about my father's life before I entered into it is the paraphernalia we found in two boxes in a closet shortly after he died. This treasure trove contained loose photographs, an album, letters, invitations, newspaper clippings, a journal of his time in the navy,

dance cards, and programs of plays he acted in from school and college.
I have never thrown them out. Over the years I have done some weed-
ing—finding pictures of people I could not identify, short notes that had
no context—but much I have held onto, feeling that it was evidence of the
kind of the life that Eddie liked remembering he had lived.

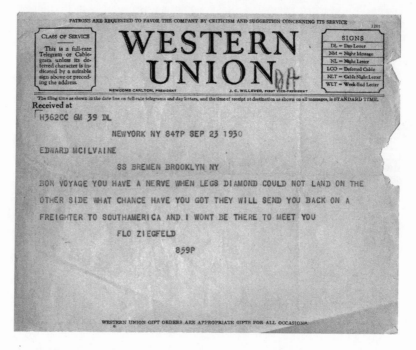

Eddie was an eligible bachelor who had a knack for making people
laugh. His life was occasionally serious, but consistently social, tinged
with celebrities from the Jazz Age as it transitioned from the twenties to the thirties, some names still familiar: J.P. Morgan, Irving Berlin, Gene Tunney, Alexander Calder, Maurice Chevalier. Eddie seems
to have known Rita Hayworth, spoken with Joseph Conrad, and met
queens and future kings at parties. Years later, I would meet the Duke of
Windsor at a nightclub in Palm Beach. Someone had decided it would
be a good idea for my brother David and me to go out to dinner and
dance with Charlotte and Anne Ford. I was about twelve at the time,
my father was the host, and on the way out we ran into the former king
and his wife, both of whom wondered aloud if we weren't a little young
for the scene, a little unfair as we had arrived so early that we had been
the scene.

Pictures show Eddie as a young and handsome forty-year-old. At ease in social situations, he was a good dancer, made witty remarks, loved life, and fell in love with my mother. His twenty-year advantage had to have been a kind of plus for her; she would have seen herself as too grown up for college students, and she would not have found men who were focused on beginning their careers sufficiently dazzling. She must have loved being adored and he must have loved adoring her. He was likely seduced, after all his years of wandering, by the chance to reinvent himself with someone so fresh and young and passionate.

They were married at Cobb Cottage. It was a September wedding and judging by the guest book that reads like a Who's Who of the day, no one they knew had anything else to do. The groom was sent off with an elaborate bachelor's party at "21" as if it was the end of an era. His bride waited for him, I suspect pleased that her husband-to-be had so many friends. I have no idea how Seebee, who had known Eddie McIlvain long before my mother did, felt about her daughter's choice, but she obviously did not stint on the reception.

My father's father, also Edward (but never Eddie), had passed his considerable girth onto his only child. Edward McIlvain had been a successful businessman, first as the president of Bethlehem Steel until Charles Schwab decided otherwise, and later as the person responsible for man-

aging annexed "alien" (German) properties during World War I. Edward
died before I was born. His father before him, William McIlvain, also a
success in business, was a burgher of Reading, Pennsylvania. His reputation as a great hiker is attested to by a pavilion erected in his name in 1892
at a spot where he liked to stop when exploring Neversink Mountain.

This has to be a picture of my father Eddie, mysteriously wearing a tie,
fishing with my grandfather.

McIlvains have been in this country since 1740 when a certain James
McIlvain, whose father had left Scotland near the turn of the century, em-
igrated from County Antim in Ireland to Delaware County with his wife
and six children. McIlvains seemed to be fairly successful entrepreneurs and
have proved fairly easy to trace. One married a granddaughter of John Morton, a signer of the Declaration of Independence and the source of my name.
I was around the age of seven when I went on a pilgrimage to the Morton
homestead where I was told he'd grown up. I marveled at what I was assured
was his toothbrush and signed my name with pride in the guest book. I
thought it was a very small house. I saw his headstone in a nearby graveyard.

My father's mother Amy's family house is not so small, but is also
historic. Wye Farm on Maryland's Eastern Shore has been linked to her
mother's family, the Lloyds, since the seventeenth century. It is still occupied and is currently owned by a descendant of its original owner, Edward Lloyd. It has had a long and complex history. I did not know of its

existence until my father took me there when I was twenty, shortly after my friend Melzie died. I knew that some of the seven first cousins on his mother's side had lived around Baltimore. I was going to college at Johns Hopkins and had met and dined with one of those cousins, but in general his Maryland connection was a mystery to me. During our weekend at Wye, I learned that his own memories of the Eastern Shore were painful, mainly because his grandparents' house, Waverly, had been destroyed in a fire.

The weekend at Wye was a revelation to me. I felt welcomed as a member of a family I'd always belonged to but had never known. I learned the history of the house and read a treasured letter from a guest who had been treated badly in the 1820s. It hung on a wall to remind the Lloyds to be gracious. For the first time, I ate oysters on the half shell (I had to muster the courage) and was amazed to find I liked them. We had terrapin from the shores of the Wye River and beef (rather stringy) from Wye Angus. Morgan Schiller, who had married my father's cousin, Elizabeth Lloyd, had resigned his banking job with Mellon in Pittsburgh to become a farmer. I met Bunny Lloyd, another cousin, who apparently had had to struggle financially much of his life, and heard the story of his two children. Everyone had thought they were oblivious to the sacrifices their parents had made for them, but they had just given their parents a trip to Europe as an anniversary present.

One day during my visit, I remember going to lunch at a friend's mansion where the footmen were in livery and we were served tiny portions of Brunswick stew. In the car on the way back to Wye, I realized I had loved feeling included in the gentle laughter at the pretention of it all, loved the unaffected nature of my relatives, the lack of pomp, the comfort they found with being who they were. I remember sitting in the farm's office and enjoying a sense of how important it was to the Schillers that the farm be a working farm, not an ornament. "Actually," Morgan said, "we have no choice. We could never afford to live here without Wye's being able to sustain itself."

Out behind the house, where you might expect to find a patio, was the history of the Lloyds in stone: a large family graveyard was stocked with graves and the tombs of relatives, some of whom seemed to invite you to sit and ruminate about the lives they had lived. The dates on the stones stretched back before the Civil War to a time when the plantation was vast and included hundreds of slaves. I had always taken a kind of pride in my Northern heritage. I liked to think that my family had not been involved with the slave trade. I understood that some of my ironmonger McIlvain relatives had stood strong against slavery and that the boilerplate they made had gone down on the Monitor. Whatever ancestors of mine who fought in the Civil War had fought on the Union side; whoever had died had died for the Union cause.

My grandmother Amy had told me Br'er Rabbit and Br'er Fox stories in the New York apartment she lived in that later became my father's. Her voice was soft and southern, but Maryland had been on our side in the Civil War, and despite the American history I had absorbed in school, it never registered with me that it had been a slave state. I felt somewhat humbled by the knowledge, and also somewhat startled by the poverty that seemed to line the roads on the Eastern Shore. Small black churches, and between them fragile, paint stripped huts, clustered here and there.

Now they are excavating at Wye, acknowledging and uncovering the history. In some ways they haven't had much choice, as the most famous resident of Wye was, in fact, a slave. I learned this long after my visit when reading *The Autobiography of Frederick Douglass*. I was astonished to read that he had returned to Wye in the 1870s to have a drink with the Lloyds on the veranda. Douglass describes going to meet with one of the daughters of Colonel Lloyd, whom he had last seen as "a slender young lady of 18.... She invited me to a seat, introduced me to her grandchildren, conversed with me as freely and with as little embarrassment as if I had been an old acquaintance." When he left, "a beautiful little granddaughter of hers, with a pleasant smile on her face, handed me a bouquet of ma- ny-colored flowers." I decided to believe that "little granddaughter" was my grandmother.

Later, I wrote a poem about Wye that ends:

My grandmother as a child
brings summer to the elevated man
(a bouquet of many-colored flowers)
whom her grandmother as a
child had known as Freddy
her father's foreman's slave
the yellow boy who later ran away
inviting him to sit here by her side
this old acquaintance of equal station
and the two adults sharing
a new dawn in the sunset of decay
memories from which the years had
sloughed the violence but not

the tears which gather for them both,
before a sudden gust of laughter
has vanquished sentiment.

We are all the child they dreamed of;
We are none;
Each lives in this unfinished mansion,
Cast in a closet or a suite;
On nights you hear the rusty hinges sigh,
We're gliding past Wye's shutters into sky.

When I knew him, my father was a vice president of "21" Brands, a whole-sale liquor distributor that was a post prohibition outgrowth of the "21" Club. He seemed to be responsible for wines (I remember Louis Martini and Wente Brothers) and champagne (Roederer and Korbel). Once on a break from boarding school, I went with him when he tried to convince a wholesaler to take on more of their line or spirits than Ballantine's Scotch. My mother's sister Suzanne's husband, my uncle Charlie, who would have known, said my father was an excellent soft-salesman, but I could not tell. I just wanted him to close the deal so we could get to lunch.

I remember his office well. It was a wonderful, spacious room. He was going to it on the day he died. After we'd shared breakfast that morning, he had a heart attack when he tried to get out of the taxi that had taken him to work. An hour later I was sitting at his desk, going through papers, his secretary Gloria guiding me. I have always treasured having that last breakfast with him. We had gone out to dinner at The River Club the night before—it was in the building I had grown up in—with my god-father, Roland Harriman. The occasion was a belated celebration of my twenty-first birthday that included a check for $1000, which I showed my father in the morning. The next day he was going to take my brother David and me on a trip across the country.

My mother would live for another forty-nine years. Toward the end of her life, like her mother, she had dementia. In some ways I grew closer to her then than I ever had, talking to her, as did my sister Sydney, virtu-ally every day. Before she died, I wrote this poem that I read at her funeral.

Talking to My Mother at 92

Her voice has never changed.
Stokowski, flirting I suspect,
Praised its deep timbre, wanted to arrange
For her to sing. Reminded, she pretends

A memory. Each night
We talk, in words unsullied by
Connections, words unfailingly polite.
Some, Maine, places in general, many names

Once quite familiar, have
Vanished in the havoc of her past.
And yet she'll recognize my voice and laugh
When I announce my dog has rediscovered mud.

Then she'll say she loves me,
And I will echo what she says.
She must find comfort in those words now free
Of history, as if, with so much loss,

Friends, husbands, sisters, Ed,
My brother killed in Vietnam,
Long buried feelings needed to be said.
Why not abandon reticence when you

Stop registering time,
And every moment seems to bleed
Into a wash of yesterdays, each line
Of waves just like the next, their shapes collapsed

Reformed, endless self
Mimicry, vague and borderless?
I choose to prattle on: I'm fine, my health
Is good, I have a cocktail, too. I list

The highlights of my day
And she responds, at times with wit;
The art of conversation still remains,
Unfazed by life's confusion. It's been

An hour since I pruned
A rose and moved it in the garden.
Now, she applauds my efforts and uproots
This memory: again, we're driving by

The dark, manured fields
Of Kennett Square to Jennersville;
We pick up roses—Mr. Lincoln, Peace,
New Yorker, Mme Chaing Kai-shek, stark,

So thorny that I fear
To carry them. Why not park them
In the entry, beneath the chandelier?
No! Just kidding! Later, digging deep

Into the loam . . . It was
The first real work I'd ever done.
We planted them, together, when she was
Not yet forty and I was seventeen.

Badeau, neé M'am'selle Sutor, was all but grafted onto the family tree.

M'AM'SELLES

Peggy was only twenty-three when I was born, while Eddie was for-ty-four. I picture him, an only child, decades away from his childhood, in an age where fathers stood on the periphery of child raising, hovering around at the birth with a puzzled expression on his face. It was an expression Peggy probably shared. She told me years later that she had no idea what she was doing when I came along. Having a baby nurse and then a governess—a "m'am'selle"—was all she had known as a child, and it was what she expected to have with her own children. It was the only model available.

The model had not fostered a happy childhood for Peggy. Her relationship with her mother, who stated more than once that children were to be seen and not heard, had been distant. Seebee admitted that her third daughter Edith, known as Teddie, had written on a college application, "I met my mother when I was seventeen." Peggy felt much closer to her sister Suzanne than she ever did to Seebee, who was as warm and welcoming to us (we knew when to be quiet) as she was aloof with her own children. Neither she nor my mother was ever "Mom" to her children.

"Did Mother ever give you a hug?" Aunt Suzie, at eighty-seven, asked my mother.

"No," my mother, ninety, responded, "I don't think she did."

We onlookers—my brother David, his daughter Wendy, my wife Betsy, Marise (the woman who was then looking after my mother, her own M'am'selle at the end of her life) and I—applauded their embrace. When you are a child, you know only the world into which you are born. It never occurs to you that your family is not every family, that its idiosyncrasies are not universal. You need to discover your place in the community. You try to belong.

Mine is the story of someone who was brought up by many, many m'am'selles. The governesses were always there in the evening to tuck us

in, as well as in the morning to wake us. They parade in front of me as I
think on them, a varied band, an assortment worthy of a Whitman's Sam-
pler, bedecked in starched white uniforms or lavender dresses appliquéd
with everything from peonies to bicycles. Some were American, some English, some German, some French. The last was Irish, the most treasured
Swiss. There were Misses and Frauleins, but they all reach me now as
m'am'selles, their collective accent French. They stood apart from the
other servants who were always part of the household, often in considerable numbers. Because she depended upon an allowance extended to
her by her mother, my mother never had as many servants to keep track
of, but she had plenty.

I have no recollection of the first m'am'selle—a proud woman who
quit after witnessing my being given champagne at my christening. Apparently she curled my hair, for the day before she left was the last one on
which I sported ringlets. Pictures show me happy enough, though I understand she force-fed me spinach, holding my nose until I opened my mouth
and, after a gasp, giving the spoon an opportunity. My mother, who was
a recent refugee from her own childhood, later confessed she had no idea
what to do; she was horrified by my gargled screams, but too intimidated
by this sergeant major to act on my behalf.

A second m'am'selle, this one in a nurse's uniform, breaks ranks and
moves about the room like an egret. In her left hand, extended about as
far from her uplifted nostrils as possible, is a diaper, in her right hand a toy
that had been left in the doorway so that surely she would have stepped
on it and fallen, shattering one of her brittle legs, if she hadn't long had
a sixth sense about such things. This is Miss Proudfoot, a proper nanny,
not to be confused with Miss Broadfoot, a puddle duck of a woman who
never reached the pond, but chose instead to waddle between my brothers
and me, quacking orders like a domineering aunt in a Disney cartoon. Oh,
didn't David and I wreak our revenge when we hammered at her with
our little fists and drove her from our room? Our outbreak occurred on a
weekend morning during a span of two weeks when she had been placed in
charge of our lives while our mother and stepfather were skiing in Europe.
How astonished we were at our sudden power, a power we knew would
be short lived, that awareness alone causing its collapse and hastening our
retreat into the bathroom where the locked door served to protect us until
hunger brought us out to our stern but somehow understanding guardian.

There is still affection in me for Miss Proudfoot, Miss Broadfoot, and
all of their cohorts, though I loved the one and tortured the other, found
a third to be kind, a fourth sadistic. Their role was to make sure we were
where we were supposed to be, to teach us manners, to send us to our room

when we were rude. One or two sang us lullabies to protect us against the night...

> *Frère Jacques, Frère Jacques,*
> *Dormez vous, dormez vous....*

The house in Mill Neck. The windows of David and my second floor room are on the left side of the center section.

I remember waking in the bedroom I shared with my brother David when I was eight, and wondering when my m'am'selle would come in to rouse us. I still can picture the shaft of sunlight that trapped dust particles, defining them, bringing them thick and numberless to a studious child who was afraid, if he blinked, that the nebula would vanish back into the invisible universe surrounding it. For an age, motionless as a mannequin, I stared at the cloud trying to pick out patterns. At first I saw none, no shape I could come close to naming, and was tempted to look at more familiar sights: a mass of freckles on my arms, the branches that I heard brushing the window in the wind, David still sleeping in the neighboring bed.

Just when I was about to turn away and banish my new world forever, I breathed something near a sigh and saw the dust in front of me stir into a wave that moved just as the waves did at the beach. Pleased, I blew a second breath and found I'd made another wave, more turbulent and scrambled, harder to discern but just as real. Again I blew, this time stretching my hand out to interrupt the air, and watched the ocean dash against a cliff. Better than trees, I thought, better than freckles, or sleeping brothers, and almost as good as the chameleons on the ceiling of the bedroom in Seebee's Palm Beach house. This was a feat of magic to rival my uncle's trick of removing his thumb only to put it back on just when you thought it was gone forever. I would have to show M'am'selle. When she came in, I would have her look and marvel.

There would come a knock on the door.

"*Bonjour!*"

"*Bonjour*, M'am'selle."

"Time to get out of bed, *mon ami.*"

"Come here, M'am'selle, come look at this."

"What is it you have there?"

"Look, I can see the air."

"Ah! In the sunlight; yes, that is nice."

"See what I can do with it?"

"And what is that?"

"Make it like waves."

"You don't say."

"Yes, see, do you see them?"

"What is that?"

"The waves."

"No, I see no waves; where are they? In the air?"

"Yes, yes, M'am'selle, I promise."

"Oh, you are fooling me, Johnny."

"No, M'am'selle, I promise."

"You boys, you are too silly. But I will tell you something. For you, my friends, I see those waves, and they are very pretty ones, but I will tell you a secret about them."

"What's that?"

"For breakfast, they are not so good."

An earlier bedroom had no windows—at least it seemed that way. Perhaps behind me there was one, its blackout blind drawn so only the slightest strip of dim light slipped through to wash gray the walls. I had been told the blind was to protect us from U-boats on the East River. I knew about U-boats from kindergarten at school where we saw newsreels about a war far away.

The dark did not frighten me, not as much as it frightened my brothers. I was the oldest and was sure the bathrobe draping the chair was just that and not a lion. Not that I was afraid of lions, no; but still, when I saw one at the zoo I shivered despite the reassurance of the thick steel bars. The roar slipped through them. I was happier with the bears, though my father had told me that a little boy had lost an arm to one just the year before. The king of beasts would not have been satisfied with anything so meager. They were more ominous than U-boats.

The lion had come nearer the bed now, as friendly as Timmy, our brown poodle. I ordered the lion to be Timmy, but that didn't work. Instead, he was telling me in his own way not to be afraid. I was too smart to be that gullible. If only I could have flown off, just flapped and been above its head, suddenly a pigeon…except cats stalk pigeons. I had seen them do so in Central Park on a Sunday morning, the same way they would stalk a parakeet free of its cage. Best to be an eagle. An eagle could soar a million miles away and still see home.

What, a voice whispers, *if there is no window? What if there is no window and you become one of the four and twenty blackbirds in a dainty pie, steaming at one end of the table? What then?*

Like a Christmas pie?

Like a Christmas pie.

They fly away.

Not this time.

Then the lion would have eaten me up and I would be gone.

Gone?

To live inside him. I thought to take a flashlight and see who was there.

Are you afraid?

Maybe.

Maybe?

There must be a window. I never heard of a room without a window.

It would be barred like the others, to keep you from falling out.

I could fly up to the ceiling and the lion, even if it stood upon my bed, could hardly catch me there.

So move your arms. Flutter them.

I can't.

The secret is not to be scared and to order it to go away. Shoo, go into the kitchen and bother Joseph.

Joseph was the butler and his hands trembled even when there were no lions. How loud his teacup would rattle if he saw a lion! But Joseph would know what to do. He would offer him a biscuit.

One of Timmy's?

No, one of his own.

Maybe the lion was a cowardly lion.

"Go on, now," I say. "Go get your biscuit."

The door opens. It is yesterday and Nana pretends to spank me so that Eddie will take his medicine. I wail my mock wail and both she and Eddie laugh at my performance.

The medicine goes down. The lion has disappeared.

Another time, Mabel, another m'am'selle, stands in the shadows of my bedroom.

"I hope I didn't wake you," she says. "I brought you Harry."

I sit up in bed to see Mabel's fiancé, the man she will leave us for. She has been our nurse for a couple of years and we love her.

"Is it nice to see Nana again?"

"Yes." Nana Proudfoot, who still moved like an egret, and had come back for a few days to nurse my mother, to whom I had given the mumps.

Harry seemed smaller than I thought he would be. We had heard so much about him. How he had been the third ranked heavyweight in the world. How he had lost his last fight because he hadn't gone to bed early enough the night before. Mabel told us how she hated to watch him fight, and that after they married he would not do that anymore. I had expected a cross between Goliath and Captain Marvel.

He was quiet. What could he say? He shook my hand and told me I had a good grip. I was half asleep, trying to think of something that would keep them there. I couldn't and Mabel said she would kiss me goodbye, but didn't want to come near because of the germs. The door closed, and the room was dark again. I heard voices in the hall and then nothing except the occasional horn bleating from the street below.

Years later, supervised by m'am'selles in brigade, I am part of a group that included my cousins Brooke and Nancy and maybe a Quintana or a Harte. We walk down the lane gingerly, our soles quick to leave the pebbles that have spilled from gravel drives onto the road. My brothers and I have invented a gait to help us traverse the stretch to the beach from Seebee's summerhouse.

This was Cobb Cottage, which Seebee had bought in the 1930s to provide her daughters with Cape Ann's sea breezes and proper Bostonian suitors in July and August. It was also the house where my father and mother had married. Said to be the oldest house on Mosconomo Street, Cobb Cottage was furnished with chintz and English country furniture, save for the entry and the library, where art deco spoke of the year Seebee bought the house—wonderful tables of odd geometric shapes, and material that the sun faded into a cubist wash over time, objects we came to know on rainy days. Seebee had added a wing that included a kitchen and above it a warren of rooms for the servants, which the m'am'selles couldn't imagine sleeping in, choosing instead to live on the third floor. At the other end, Seebee had a master bedroom built on the second floor over a porte-cochère, to which her chauffeur delivered her Rolls Royce after waxing it each morning. We would hear it stir the gravel when we visited Seebee, m'am'selle-free, while she breakfasted. The daughters' rooms contained an endless number of wardrobe closets, which became great hiding places where we would sometimes stand silently barely breathing as a m'am'selle would walk by, calling, "Boys, boys, where have you gone? It is time to go to the beach."

Grass, gravel, grass,
our bare feet skirt Cobb Avenue,
stall so we can mark how far
the morning glories fly up Mrs. Snowden's wall,
then, still uncalloused, brave the final driveway.
We catch our breath and cast our eyes
toward a Dutch door, the open half of which
belongs to Mrs. Brooks' bitch Felice.
One Great Dane bark herds us
to sanctuary, a sandy path
hemmed in against a fence by
poisoned berries hedge which blinds
Felice to us and hides us from the bees
that swarm about the summer sweet
whose scent assures us now the sea
is beckoning and has us streaking beachward.

Only to
    halt then
carefully
    descend
        the dozen
            splintery
                steps the
                    gods had
                        planted
                            there to
                                sabotage
                                    our flight.

Soles squeal down the sand like bagpipes,
flail and flicker between two waves,
pause so we may see our well-clad guardians
raise the umbrellas that rescue them from sun.
From canvas chairs they knit and jabber French,
and watch their urchins tame,
with citadels and moats halfway to China,
the furling and unfurling ocean.

We always scatter seaward
defying tales of victims of
the undertow which seems
the girlish side of waves, a sport to root our feet against,
to challenge it to cease from tossing shells amongst our toes,
to rip us toward the sea.

        It never did.
Instead, on tranquil afternoons,
we are released to swim out to a float
reserved for legends. Once there,
we loll careless as sun-warmed seals,
slipping off like seals to fish
for U-boats or the bottom of the deep.
From shore the choir of nannies
lullaby our names, but we are solely
of our time and free from theirs
and all the sun-blanched mansions on the shore
and their cries slide off us like whispers
as we gaze out to the east,
past islands held by gulls,
past the shadow of Cape Ann.

When we sailed into a dive, Castille flashed.
We saw that we could swim to Spain.
None ever tried, though as we bade the dream
farewell and raced our friends to shore,
somewhere above the hoarse surge of the waves,
the gulls kept heckling:
Dare you! Dare you! Dare you!

We dared because we knew our caretakers, who had lumbered down the splinter-laden steps that brought them from atop the dunes onto the sands, weighted with baskets and umbrellas and beach chairs, would be awaiting us. Long before they reached the spot they had chosen for their encampment, the surf was knocking us down. Barely audible m'am'selle voices called out, begging us to be careful. Words and names came drifting our way between the waves, "Watch…please…*oh la la*…undertow.… Johnny.… *Mon Dieu*.…"

Soon enough we were scooting toward them, asking if they had brought us something to drink. Having just settled back into her shaded seat and having just begun to talk in French behind her knitting, a m'am'selle would pull herself up to rummage through a basket for a thermos. Refreshed, we broke away again to swim some more. Before long, one of us had swallowed too much water, another too much sand, a third pushed a fourth after arguing about who was going back up the steps to get the raft. With every cry a m'am'selle had to rise and sigh and shuffle toward us for the rescue. Their chastisement, which accompanied the staunching of our tears, was as quickly forgotten as the rollers that had knocked us over.

After a while, though, our frolicking became less frenzied and the m'am'selles' attendance to our tragedies less frequent. The sun had snuffed the sea breeze that greeted our arrival. It climbed until its heat began to drug us. Face down we laid on towels, and our hands broke the crusted surface of the sand and then tunneled like ants. Far away our guardians drifted off, their once busy fingers folded piously over the half-finished sweaters on their laps.

The spell was broken by the tide. Unnoticed, it had pushed the sea up to our encampment. Suddenly, brought by an unannounced swell, the Atlantic introduced itself to the m'am'selles. The shouts that waked us were their orders. "Johnny, *la basket*... David, *les towels*... Brooke, *ma chaise pliante*...*" This must have been the overtow.

We sprang up, anxious to be heroes, hoping to have to swim halfway to Spain to salvage a knitting needle. But the water had subsided for a moment, and nothing had been swept away. Nothing even looked damp, except perhaps the sand the m'am'selles stood upon. Hardly discouraged, we cheerfully agreed to transplant them and their cargo. They were laughing by then, too, and we joined them, muttering nonsense syllables in imitation of their strange language and squeaking with delight at our cleverness.

When we returned to where we'd been, we found that our tunnels had been washed away. We dug frantically to reestablish them, our hands disappearing like clams and then reemerging with clumps of wet sand that seemed no more solid than the sea beside us as the turrets we attempted to form dissolved before they were built. We were losing to the ocean. We would have to retreat.

Back beside the steps we dug a giant's hole. We were using our shovels to dig beneath the bottom of the earth. We thought we could reach China. We were nearly there when it was time to return home for lunch. Emerging from our pit, still enthusiastic but hungry, we astonished our m'am'selles with our sand suits. They said, umbrellas and chairs neatly folded and piled around them, that we could clean off but pleaded for us to be quick. "Be careful," they begged as one last time we rushed to rinse ourselves in the then receding ocean.

"Last one home's a rotten..."

Off again, in the rush to be first, we funneled, squealing, into the narrow path darkened by the canopy of branches from Mrs. Brooks' hedge. It was a dingy corridor and I hated it. A bee had stung me there a week before. Remembering, I scurried wide-eyed toward the road.

"I win, I win..."

Plodding behind us, their feet securely shod, came two governesses. Wheezing slightly from our pace, between breaths, they called on us to slow down and notice the morning glories blooming on the high wall in front of Mrs. Sheldon's house. We stopped to look back at the m'am'selles in their floppy, broad-brimmed hats and their frumpish dresses that resembled tablecloths, and at the burden of baskets and umbrellas that we had rushed away from.

"Come on!" I yelled impatiently but to no avail. Stymied, I glanced at Mrs. Sheldon's morning glories and found myself captured—pale blue and white, the blossoms wavered in front of the ivy, delicately, like anchored butterflies.

Badeau, neé M'am'selle Sutor, always sat down as if, exhausted by a Himalayan expedition, she had found an easy chair in Shangri La. This act of sitting was inevitably accompanied by a sigh so rich and meaningful that it sounded more like the "Amens" in church on Easter Sunday than any kind of breathing. It was time for her to relax and have one of us bring her a hot chocolate. The ambulatory exertions to keep track of skittering children had ended for the day, and we seemed to understand that even if one of us were dangling by a shirtsleeve from a tree limb soon to be struck by lightning, he or she would have to wait until morning to be rescued. There was no need for further chasing after. Whether anyone stirred or not, the sun would rise in the morning, the birds would sing, and she would know it was time to percolate the coffee.

By my early childhood, Badeau had been all but grafted onto the family tree. She had worked first for my grandmother, bringing up my mother's two youngest sisters from scratch; then she went on to raise my cousins, Aunt Suzie's children, Brooke and Nancy. I joined her in the summers when so much of the family took advantage of the sun and the beach at Manchester, lazing the weeks away and learning to swim and play tennis. If my own m'am'selles, like comets, only seemed to stay a brief season, Badeau in August was as constant as the Dog Star. I never had to yell at her, or pummel her stomach, or tell my mother to fire her. She was someone to win over, an audience for dress up games, who laughed at our impersonations of grand ladies at tea, and who rewarded us with stories of her own.

The best were about our mothers, Peggy and Suzie, as girls. She would tell us about my mother: "How sweet a girl Peggy was, but so lazy; never have I seen such a lazy child. Why, she even had a way to open her curtains in the morning without having to leave her bed," and I would try to think if it was possible for my mother ever to have been my age. It was not. The stories were all fairytales. Aunt Suzie was always *Cher Suzanne*, a child of twelve who imitated almost everything her older sister did.

"They were at the railroad station once, and Peggy, who was very dressed up and trying to look so old and so *elegante*, dropped one of the gloves she held in her hands because it was too stylish to wear. Well, *Cher Suzanne*, who was walking behind her like a shadow, but, of course, had to do the same thing. Down went her white gloves onto that terrible floor. Then I laughed, which made them both so angry because they had gone in front of me and their little sisters, hoping no one would think that we were all together."

Badeau had a lilting voice, and the stories she told were in a light French—she would say Swiss—accent that emerged from each syllable. It gave familiar words an unfamiliar ring. Simple sentences became songs and we would sing some of the best of them over and over, late into the night, mockingbirds chanting ourselves to sleep.

The last time I saw Badeau I was in my twenties visiting my mother and stepfather in a summer villa they had rented in Formentor. There were enough steps down to the villa to tire M'am'selle, and before she had even said how beautiful the house was, set into a cliff above the Mediterranean, she found a comfortable chair to let herself sink into. She sighed as she had always sighed, but more profoundly in deference to her age and a bad left leg that acted up now and then. Before telling us of her trip or how her retirement in Switzerland was going, she admired us all and then rhapsodized on the view: the geraniums taller than we were, the blue of the sea.

She spoke with more French words than she had when I was a child but still spoke English in a way that had me whispering her version of the view to myself later. And I wanted us both to be younger again, away from that view and the cold marble floors and bleached surfaces, back in Manchester-by-the-Sea with the fading, tilting triangles on the always sandy, art deco rugs, and the wallpapers of mottled warblers. The bed with the yellow frame where I lay in sipping a ginger ale after my tonsils had come out called me home to it, and I remembered teaching a cousin, little more than half my age, the little I knew of love when I was twelve, and the gentle reprimand from Badeau when she caught me.

This m'am'selle loved us all and never had to deal with me in winter. There was no time for her to wear me out or for her to think of me as hers. I see her come to me as I stood forlorn over the scrambled eggs I was supposed to have cooked and had instead neglected. "*Oh, la,*" she says. "*C'est merveilleux. Mon cher,* you have made an omelet."

In a new Christmas outfit complete with six-shooter, I have rescued my cousin Brooke in a snow-free Grosse Pointe from the bandits Eddie and David.

In winter there were other m'am'selles and we were other selves. Christmas lunch was always at The Sycamores. We were joined in Grosse Pointe by cousins—those who had been with us in Manchester the summer before and more, as many as a baker's dozen of us all together. In bathing suits no more, we were coaxed into velvet costumes and ushered into the grand dining room, and there placed in front of doilies and gold candlesticks, which sat upon a white damask tablecloth that seemed to stretch forever. There were splendidly folded matching napkins, framed by the gleaming silver flatware, small forks, large forks, various spoons, knives, butter knives, all of which we had glimpsed being polished when we had slipped through the room the day before. In the center of each place setting rested a hand painted, gold-rimmed plate ("It is French," my grandmother said, when she noticed my interest in the bare-breasted woman dancing in the center of mine); purely decorative, these plates were taken away and new ones set down before we were served the first course and the largest of our three crystal stemware glasses were filled with water.

We found ourselves next to aunts in long gowns and uncles in blue suits, all of whom said how nice we looked, the uncles a little too loudly. Every one of them had married into the family, my grandmother and grandfather having five daughters, and they had spent the morning traipsing after my grandfather. The "Colonel," as we called Wesson Seyburn, spent most of his time on the farm in Pontiac. He had established the ritual of bringing gifts to old friends on Christmas morning. They always asked him to stay a minute. It provided him the opportunity to reconnect with his past, and to raise a glass of whisky and toast the season. The uncles, reluctant but on display, also partook. When they returned, the m'am'selles, relegated to the sidelines, frowned in disapproval. It must have given them a topic to discuss at their own Christmas lunch.

I was at one end of the table next to my grandmother, a seat of honor reserved for the eldest grandchild. I nervously eyed the apple in the pig's mouth at my grandfather's end and uttered no sound besides "Thank you" when Smith poured our ginger ale from a bottle wrapped in the same white cloth as our elders' champagne. Such exemplary children we all were, so deferential and polite that the absent m'am'selles would have barely recognized us. Except for the time Eddie's distant but clear voice, breaking the silence after the consommé had been served, asked my mother, "Who is that strange man?" His finger was pointing at the figure behind the pig. Then even the greediest among us froze our spoons and watched as my grandfather directed a withering frown at my youngest brother.

"And whose," he demanded, "little bastard is that?"

Those were the last words the Colonel spoke before he disappeared. From where I sat, I could not tell what had happened, only that he was no longer sitting there behind the pig. He had slipped from his chair as if shot. The table fell silent and the adults look confused until Seebee gestured to

Smith, and he and a footman removed my grandfather from the room. For a minute, the children, following the model of their parents and the advice of their m'am'selles, said nothing. But soon more champagne was poured, and the murmur of voices resumed, small, restrained conversations, confined to the weather and travel plans, nothing amiss until an uncle suddenly turned pale and excused himself, well before the turkey-laden dishes of the over-glazed Fitzhugh service revealed their pattern again.

In due course, upon a barely noticeable signal from my grandmother, the plates came to be removed as felicitously as her husband. I was left staring at the crumbs from the stuffing I had spilled, but instead of a *tsk-tsk* and a lecture on table manners from M'am'selle, a crumb knife in the hand of a man I had never noticed before deftly removed the debris. With the tablecloth restored, fingerbowls appeared; most of us knew enough not to drink the water but to dip our fingers into the reservoir and then move the bowls off the dessert plate. On the occasions we were permitted to eat with our parents there were also fingerbowls; only here, a servant removed the bowl. Then a plum pudding, dense with raisins and unfamiliar fruit, entered the room. We were meant to *ooh* and *aah*, but usually the flames were already extinguished, and Smith would have to call for more brandy in order for a blaze to crown the pudding. Eventually we all were provided with a small piece and were thankful that the ice cream that accompanied it was plentiful. By now the voices in the room were drifting in and out, and the clatter of silver on china rose to punctuate the conversation. We, knowing it was best not to be heard, sat hardly squirming at all, waiting politely to be set free.

What a contrast to the manic scenes in the neighboring, smaller dining room where nine or ten of us children gathered with the two or three m'am'selles to eat creamed chicken on the days leading up to Christmas. Santa was to fill our stockings, and we brayed out our cupidity in prayers for bicycles that had speedometers, electric trains that could run to San Francisco and back, and dollhouses with more rooms than the mansion we were eating in.

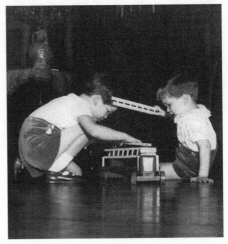

There were always toys on Christmas.

It was all the m'am'selles could do to keep us seated. They didn't even care if the carrots remained undisturbed. Although every once in a while one of us would be made aware of the starving children of Abyssinia, the governesses had learned to restrain their compulsion for clean plates. Their nature had been curbed by the company of fellow m'am'selles, and the prospect that our potential outcry would reach my grandfather's ears, causing him to come thundering into the room, ordering their heads to be placed on a platter or threatening to withhold the handkerchiefs he was planning to present on Christmas Day.

The family gathers at Seebee's for Christmas. Brooke, David, the author, and Eddie sit left to right on the bottom row. My cousin Linda is in her father's arms. Only the Colonel is absent.

What a fearsome giant of a man he seemed to us all: still "the Colonel" even thirty years after leaving the army. He liked me because I did not want to go to Yale (his alma mater) or Princeton (my father's) or Harvard (two of my uncles'). He approved of my desire to be an engineer. That conversation would have taken place early in the day, well before lunch and the fortifying pre-lunch. Outside the windows the snow would whirl toward us off the lake, and we would shout to be released into it so we could stab each other with icicles and hide behind colonnades, waiting to humble our enemies by ambushing them under an avalanche.

There was one other season in Grosse Pointe; one when my grandfather was safely exiled to his farm in Pontiac, one when my brothers and I were left to the whims of M'am'selle (Fraulein) Van Snyck without the buffer of cousins and with only the distant beneficence of my grandmother to protect us. It was May, two months yet before we'd strike out for Massachusetts, and the trees we had only known as skeletons were in full leaf. The walled garden that had been our Arctic fortress was as exotic as Tarzan's backyard. The lake we had all walked on thinking we might reach Canada now would support only boats. We had been remanded to Eden while my mother went to Idaho for her divorce. We had no idea what divorce was, only that there would be change.

The lima beans were thick, jaundiced, and unfamiliar. They lay unsuccessfully hidden by my knife and fork. I had hoped that my brothers would have dealt with the vegetables as I had, but they had betrayed me. I had forgotten that even if they had mimicked me, there is never safety in numbers for the oldest. The oldest must set an example; something M'am'selle hinted at as she asked me when I was planning to finish my meal.

"When David does."

"I did better than you did."

"You didn't have as much to start with."

"Yes I did."

"Boys, I don't understand this. Such good beans."

"But, I don't like them."

"Me neither."

"I have never heard of such a thing."

She speared some lima beans with a fork and moved them toward my unopened mouth. I tried to focus on them, hoping to convince myself they looked like peas. Peas weren't so bad. They could be small and sweet and they made rice better. But these weren't peas and weren't about to become them. No, lima beans insisted on their own unsquished identity—sallow, unyielding, and kidney shaped. Tears welled in my eyes. M'am'selle permitted a few of them to roll down my cheeks until she expressed astonishment at their presence.

"So much fuss over such a small mouthful. What kind of a man will you ever be? A big, strong man is what I hope because of an empty plate."

The fork hadn't moved so I didn't dare answer. She tried to console me using soft words, telling stories of famous men who had eaten lima beans, starting with "players of baseball" and working back to "the great Alexander." In my dreams I might become as glorious as any of them, but as long as that clotted fork remained in position my mouth remained shut.

Smith came in to clear the table. M'am'selle greeted him by explaining that my place, at least, would have to remain set. It seemed I was not hungry yet and would need to wait awhile before I ate.

Smith laughed. "Well, Johnny, I cannot see why you wouldn't want these beans here. I picked them with my two hands this morning. Look. I think they're still a little green."

I looked at his hands but saw nothing but pinkish flesh.

"No, they are not," I spluttered.

Smith looked at his hands himself, and then said in astonishment, "Well, how could that be? I could have sworn on *The Book of Common Prayer* that they were as green as a frog. Indeed, I thought they were frogs."

He dropped his right hand on the table beside my placemat and it sprang up. "See, there it goes."

I laughed, in spite of feeling too old for such tricks and knowing I was being bribed.

"Will you do me a big favor now, Johnny, and eat so I can clear the table and bring you some ice cream?"

I nodded in solemn agreement, squinted, and opened my mouth. M'am'selle Van Snyck obliged.

"See how good they are, my child."

I tried with all my might to agree with her, but by this time they were cold, and whatever goodness they had once possessed was gone forever. Still, I chewed dutifully. Trying to think ahead to the ice cream, I struggled to triumph, my teeth battling, my fingers crossed, my heart hopeful until another forkful headed toward me. Panicked, I went blind and started counting. At six I took a deep breath, held it, and willed myself to swallow. I opened my eyes, looking for my glass of milk, but Smith had taken it away. The mashed remnants of my chewing reappeared involuntarily on the plate in front of me.

M'am'selle, shocked, shrieked something in German. Eddie began to cry. David, perhaps hoping for anther frog, looked at a hastily retreating Smith.

"You are a wicked boy," M'am'selle Van Snyck hissed at me like a snake from my most dreaded nightmare. "You must go to your room. When you are ready to have these beans at supper you will learn how good they are."

Rubbing the tears from my eyes and the sting from my fanny, I gladly fled, the distant threat barely a cloud, out of the breakfast room, through the dining room, opening its heavy doors into the living room, and taking a quick right into the front hall. Then up, up. By the time I reached the top of the staircase, I knew only that I had escaped and had been given over to myself. I would miss the afternoon walk that followed the vinegar bath to protect me from the mosquitoes. Instead, I could sneak about my grandmother's house, exploring rooms, drawing curtains, discovering bathrooms with faucets that poured forth a little rust before the water cleared. Or when I knew M'am'selle was outside with my brothers, I could sneak into the bathroom and pour out the scented lotions she kept on a shelf, or cross the hall to her room and put a rubber spider under her pillow.

For ten minutes I laid in exile on my bed and stared at the clock's stubbornly still hands. Then I tried to count to one thousand. At three hundred eleven I scaled the wallpaper, discovering three different kinds of flowers before the pink rose repeated itself. That was going up. Across it was only one. I sat up and let my fingers hop from one rose to another; higher and higher they rose, trying not to be trapped in the thistle where a praying mantis lay patiently waiting, its pincers trembling.

"See there, monkey face, you can't catch me."

"Why's that, squirt head?"

"Because I'm too fast."

Swiftly and unannounced, the mantis strikes, pulling the grasshopper off the wall and thrashing it into stillness on the bed.

A noise from above made me look up. Perhaps to taunt me, my brothers have been taken to the ballroom on the third floor and were allowed to romp around, forcing long dormant dust balls to stir and dance a jitterbug across the parquet. I listened for more footsteps but heard none and wondered if David and Eddie were playing a game with the Punch and Judy puppets. We had found them two days earlier, under a sheet in a decaying box our mother might have packed them in twenty years before. We would have had them chase each other from one end of the room to the other, but their strings were so entangled that they could only hobble like one-legged soldiers lurching down hospital corridors.

My fingers stirred in imitation, skipping their way across my chest. I heard no more sounds from above. What if what I had heard was only a detachment of mice scouting the upper reaches of their kingdom?

Looking out the window toward the lake, I saw sailboats gliding as swiftly as skates had in winter. I remembered trying to show off, jumping onto the ice from a snow bank and cutting my chin badly enough for stitches. How I screamed when the doctor came toward me with his needle! The family had gathered about telling me how brave I was, but I knew that was a lie.

David, Eddie and I on the gravel path of my grandmother's garden in Grosse Pointe the year Eddie and Peggy divorced. When in Grosse Pointe, Seebee's grandchildren were often photographed to appear in the "Style" section of the Detroit Free Press.

It was only two o'clock. The day stretched beyond me farther than the lake. It stopped at Canada, but I might have to serve out my sentence forever. How many hours in a day? How many minutes in an hour? How many seconds in a minute? In my mind, I battled time and dullness by trying to calculate the number of ticks the clock would make before I died. I got lost in the three hundred thousands but felt safe there.

Two-fifteen. They had forgotten me. Now, it was time to go slip outside. I rose and went to the door, quietly turning the handle, only to discover it had been locked from the outside. No! M'am'selle could not keep

me in the whole afternoon. Seebee would save me. She always liked to
have me in the morning room for cards. Between bids and tea sandwiches,
Seebee's friend Mrs. McGivern would compliment her on having such a
polite grandson. I was a little boy in a blue checkered shirt that matched
the light blue of my shorts. I could have stepped out from behind the lady
reading a book in the Renoir over the fireplace in the living room. When
Smith left the room, I was allowed to pass the tray to Mrs. McGivern who
liked to remind me of the time we played Oklahoma together and who
shuffled cards so they fluttered in her hands like hummingbird wings.

Two-thirty. I was longing for a deck of cards so I could play solitaire.
I discovered that toothpaste used as shaving cream stings; that there were
one hundred seventeen books in the bookcase; that I was able to recall
almost every word of "The House That Jack Built."

When she finally came back, m'am'selle Van Snyck greeted me with
a smile. It was as if nothing had ever happened. "You must come outside
right now," she said. "Your brothers are waiting for you. Quick, *quick.*"

One afternoon I did get to escape completely. I was sent to a baseball game
with George Bach, a chauffeur who had been with Seebee ever since he
had been "given" to her by her father as a present for her eighteenth birthday. A kind and crinkled gentleman, George Bach was missing a thumb.
Countless times he told us it had happened in the war, that he had come
too near an airplane propeller—we would shout that the last time he'd said
his thumb had been shot off by a sniper.

On the day of the game I would not have cared if it had been my
thumb that was gone. As the car (it must have been his own, and not Seebee's limousine with the fur blanket in the back where I had to ride) left
the solemn gray stones, the grand house receding in its rear view mirror,
I underwent a metamorphosis. The sullen child, who the combination of
the tyranny of M'am'selle Van Snyck and the absence of my mother and
father had made mute, became an unwinding chatterbox who not only
announced the batting average of half the American League but also sang
"The Star Spangled Banner" and "Take Me Out to the Ballgame" on the
way to Briggs Stadium. The Tigers and Hal Newhouser were going to
scalp the Indians, and I was going to be there to celebrate.

During the warm-ups George Bach taught me how to keep score. As
soon as the first Indian batter came to the plate I was ready for him to
strike out so I could record the fact for posterity. He did not cooperate
and neither did his teammates, especially Bob Feller, who forced me to
write a "k" beside the name of too many of my champions. I joined in the
rhythmic clapping, cheered madly at every fly ball the Tigers managed,

stood at the bottom of the seventh; but, nothing I did had the power to turn the tide. By the bottom of the ninth I was hoarse and slightly crestfallen. All the way home I jabbered about what would have happened if only Hoot Gibson hadn't struck out in the sixth.

My brothers, deemed too young for the outing, greeted me on my return as if I were Ty Cobb. Even M'am'selle was solicitous until she heard me boast, first of a Coke and then of a hot dog and finally of a popsicle that George Bach had bought me. The scowl descending her reddened face should have warned me to retreat. She had forbidden me to have anything but water. Though she would have found me out eventually, this was the worst possible way. I was flaunting my disobedience, waving a red flag, goading the Minotaur into charging.

Walking backward, I tried to explain. "Seebee said I could; she said I could. I asked her."

This was a mistake, for I had gone over M'am'selle's head, adding impertinence to my defiance. My defense was either not believed or unacceptable. Down I went, squalling; up I came double squalling, dragged thumping to my room, her strength more pointed than my yowling, her turning of the key more effective than my rattling of the handle.

"Stop that!" she was saying. "You must not disobey. I have never heard such disobedience. I have never had such a problem as you are. So nasty a boy you have been."

As I lay on the bed, face buried, eyes wet with humiliation and pain, I shuddered with hatred, muttering my revenge between sobs.

"You are a bad boy," she said a final time, more gently but with conviction.

Alas for M'am'selle, her victory was short-lived. She had miscalculated. Seebee was not one to deny her grandchildren indulgences. After all, she had a few of her own. Even then I knew the story of her ringing Smith's predecessor Osborne to ask him if she had had lunch.

"Yes, madam."

"Well, I don't remember it. Let's have it again."

And she did. There was no way this woman, our Seebee, her very name probably a grandchild's mispronunciation of her last name Seyburn, would not have sympathized with this grandchild's tale of woe.

She had sent me to the baseball game, and as soon as she had returned from her round of golf, she wanted to see me. I was escorted to her sitting room by Betty, her personal maid, who drew my grandmother's baths and laughed at me in the mornings when I helped my grandmother choose what she might wear that day from the astonishing array of dresses in her closet-lined dressing room.

Seebee had expected a boy who couldn't contain himself, who described each pitch in detail and showed her how Newhouser twisted his wrist when he threw a curve.

"But M'am'selle put me in my room, and you said it wasn't fair if I didn't have a Coke, but M'am'selle put me in my room."

My grandmother wiped the tear from my eye and reminded me that at seven I was almost too old to cry. She said that it was all right. M'am'selle would not be locking me away any longer. She would see to it, and, of course, I was allowed to have that Coke. She had even given George Bach a dollar to make sure I would get one.

"Now, tell me about the game."

I recounted the tale of woe.

"Oh, no!"

"Yes. But I learned how to keep score. Look, here's the scorecard. The "k's" stand for strikeouts. And see those lines. Those were hits."

"It looks like Newhouser had a long day."

"He wasn't too good, at least after the second inning. But you should have seen…"

M'am'selle hung on a little while longer but was never quite the same after that. A little food could be left on a plate without comment and we were able to laugh and even giggle without reprimand. She took us back to our new home on Long Island and stayed until one summery morning when our mother discovered that the only times M'am'selle liked to encourage our play was when we were naked. She would sit on a chair near the tennis court and urge us to scamper about until we dropped, panting like three worn-out nymphs ringing an approving Diana. We did not mind except when the bees swarmed in the clover, or when a sprinkler's placement meant that we had to dart through cold water, but our mother coming across these revels one morning could not believe her eyes. M'am'selle had to pack up and depart with her fine references and her refined peccadilloes.

M'am'selle Van Snyck had been hired to look after three children whose parents were being divorced and take them from New York to Detroit, a city where she had never been, in a part of the world she could never have imagined as a child. She had grown up expecting to be just like her mother, raising her own *fils et filles* in the same small village with its "worth a visit" church, its stone walls, and meandering river. But instead she went to work—it would have been during the Depression— ironing sheets and daydreaming of her sisters as she scrubbed floors, her childhood out of reach. Before the war came she would have reached America with references. Perhaps she helped raise an officer's children while he was off fighting her people—no, she must have been Swiss German or Austrian.

Then she'd found herself travelling westward through the night on the *Wolveriner*, hurtling toward the American heartland, not tempted to join me as I raised the shade to watch the surrounding towns and countryside pass by, not a bit entranced by the clacking of the wheels below or the magical blue hue of the nightlight above. She steeled herself against the haunting whistles of the train and didn't blink when a rival train just missed us as it thundered past, rushing toward New York. She never saw the sightless headlights of the cars staring at us at crossroads or ask about their owners, old and young, some mad at us for slowing down their trip, lonely and anxious to be home, others smiling at the interruption, remembering the nights they had spent looking out like I did at the fascinating dark.

On the lawn at Manchester where their wedding portrait was taken, a
family portrait eight months before Peggy divorced Eddie.

The farm at Kent.

KENT

In my late thirties I found myself walking from a bus stop in Middletown, Connecticut, to an Arco station a mile and a half down Route 66, near where, a week before, my VW Bus had sputtered to a stop. Stiff from three hours aboard a Trailways bus, I had convinced myself I would enjoy the walk from the depot to my car. It had been repaired, and I was back to bring it home to New Jersey.

The brisk air, a touch of January in October, dispelled the stupor induced by the overheated bus. Revived enough to feel like jogging, I took off up a long hill leaving the town behind me. The houses that I passed appeared to be Victorian victims of a widened road, most of their once proud facades dingy and disfigured. Maybe that was why instead of admiring the final flaring of the large maple ahead of me, my mind wandered to the smoky waiting room of the Port Authority where I had spent a good part of the morning pretending to read *Herzog* while listening to one of the permanent residents who was expatiating, in foul language, on Ford, Carter, and the state of the world. As I left one derelict behind, another replaced him. This fellow, also reeking of whisky, had entered the bus in New Rochelle on crutches. He moved to the back seats and started to hold court there, announcing to the nearest rider, a young black man trying to get to Boston, that he had had his toes shot off by a shotgun. "But the guy who did it…you should see what I did to him. He's in worse shape, much worse. Yes, he is."

Terrible shape—I could relate. I slowed to a wobbly walk at the maple, gasping a bit, surprised at how few yards I'd managed to run before becoming so winded. I played competitive squash, and it had been four years since I had smoked my last cigarette. At least there were no witnesses. When I reached the crest of the hill, the wind picked up and stung my face, chasing off the rest of my day and making me feel glad that I had exerted enough energy to keep from getting a chill. I tried to think how far it was to the Arco station. I thought I would have seen it by now. I told myself I should have asked what the final damage for the repair would be. But it was too nice an afternoon to dwell on my carelessness and suddenly I caught the scent of burning leaves.

The air told me I had been here before.

"Dad, can I light this match?"

"No. Now just stand back a little."

"Is this all right?"

"Yes, that's good. We'll just get this underway, and we'll be cooking on the front burner."

"It's smoking."

"There it goes."

"Can I rake the fire into the next pile?"

"In a minute, but be careful... Stand over here. That's it... Not too quickly..."

I was back in Kent under the same clear Connecticut sky, the sun close enough to make me forget the sharpening breeze threatening the leaves that were not burning. It made no difference that the highway beside me was filled with cars and trucks racing by. They failed to throttle memories of the dirt road I had walked on so many years before, of kicking the same mica-flecked rock all the way from the Longwells' house to ours. When I stopped on the small wooden bridge that crossed the brook, it meant I was home.

I looked down and watched the water flash gaily under me. In the eddies at the side I could see the mottled bark of a buttonwood tree glistening beneath a cloud that burst upon a rock and tumbled acrobatically into the shadows. Then, I walked on. I reached a railroad trestle and spotted the Arco sign beyond. "Time to sprint," I said to myself, shaking loose the freshet, forgetting the stone.

My life at Kent predates my memories of it. Kent was part of my mother and father's happiest times, where they went when they escaped the city and acted like landed gentry. For them it was a summer place, a place to visit and relax and be part of a world that was only a few hours from New York, but seemed to belong to another realm, a rural wonderland to which their friends would flock for idle weekends.

I was christened in Kent. This seems to have been a major event or at least a good excuse for a party. I was toasted and celebrated. In addition

to my parents, the occasion attracted godparents, aunts, uncles, and miniature schnauzers I don't recall, all of whom gathered on the lawn and were
observed critically no doubt by the m'am'selle who would quit the next day.
It was just before the younger men would be going off to war (at forty-five,
my father was told he was too old). A bright interval in a darkening time.

My grandmother McIlvain and the minister who christened me at Kent.

After my parents divorced, my father held onto his farm at Kent for
three or four years before selling it. After Kent was gone, he took us to
places where he rented rooms, usually Southampton, or he chartered a
yacht for a cruise, usually between Newport and Manchester. The summer
I turned fourteen, he leased an apartment carved out of a Newport mansion aptly named Beachmound, which became our new Kent, and though
it included some of the furniture from the farm, I have never let go of the
original.

My times at Kent have affected me deeply. I loved, and still do love,
the idea that my father kept it just for us. When I separated from my first
wife, I bought a house in Maine so our boys would have somewhere to be
with me. It was a modest summer cottage, which I have held onto through
times when it made no financial sense to do so, but when the thought of
not having it left me empty and disoriented. Now my wife Betsy and I are
here year round. Between the two of us, we have lived in over forty differ-

ent places, but we have shared this one for more than a quarter of a century. The house has been insulated and expanded over the years; our children come back tolerant of the changes, and our grandchildren have started to visit. It has answered my longing for Kent, for a home where I could be as good a father as my own.

We never lived in Kent, though—we visited. Our father took David and me and sometimes Eddie there on weekends in the summer and the fall, free from M'am'selles. In the years before I turned eleven, I watched every summer come to its end at Kent, first with a blaze, and then with a few stains that echoed the rust and rot of the door leading into the long abandoned barn, where David and I crossed shaky timbers toward a pile of forgotten tools in a far corner. A nearly toothless harrow lay beside a spinning wheel that didn't spin, half of its spokes scattered about our feet. Atop a plow was propped a weathered Windsor chair. The spinner might have sat upon it once, spinning the wool she would later weave into the fabric for a winter skirt. We looked about for an old trunk, hoping to find the skirt and more. Our visions of lost treasure battled my father's voice, which called us in for lunch. David and I decided we better go. It was not worth risking Dad's wrath for just a scrap of cloth or even gold.

Outside it always seemed much colder on those early fall days at Kent. The wind numbed our hands and we ran toward the house yelling, "Coming!" In the kitchen we let the steam from hot soup warm our faces. We were chided about the mud we had brought into the hall, but as we looked at our father we knew he was not really angry. Behind him, out the window, a sudden gust blew a storm of leaves across the lawn. We heard some shutters rattle. I took a sip of tomato soup and thought of the fire in the living room and felt safe from winter.

Our trips to Kent began late on Friday afternoons when our father picked us up and drove the three hours there from Long Island in a gray 1941 Desoto that still boasted my mother's former initials, PSM, on its Connecticut plates. It turned dark long before we arrived, and the lights on the dashboard, a novelty to someone used only to daylight travels, entranced me. Eyeing them, I steered with an imaginary wheel. I always got to ride in the front seat and only lost my focus when David and Eddie broke out into one of their inevitable wars and we pulled over at last, my foot on an imaginary brake, so my father could turn around and shout at them.

A sandwich by the road was our dinner, one made by his housekeeper Lizzie—bacon, if we were lucky—and when we arrived we were hustled off to bed. Under huge comforters, we slipped off to sleep, wondering about the Iroquois. The windows on the second story were less than a foot high, and we had been told that the settlers, after shuttering the first floor, stuck their rifles through them when the Indians attacked. For proof, there were arrowheads around; when we found one, we slipped it under the pillow to protect us from the night.

I guess today I find myself reluctantly supposing the windows had been made so small to conserve heat. But the old part of the white clapboard house did date from the eighteenth century, and the farm was far enough from any other to make it a likely target for raid, if any such raids took place. Set in the corner of a small valley, the cluster of Kent's buildings was shadowed in the afternoon by a high hill we called a mountain. In front ran the brook and quite far beyond that lay the fields. It must have been the valley's water that attracted the pioneer. It is hard to see what else would have brought him so far from the main road. Perhaps he liked the idea of crossing the small bridge at night and leaving all that work on the other side.

His heir was the tenant who lived down past the Longwells and whose barn was near his home and was very different from the dilapidated one David and I liked to explore. Walking there, seeking other adventure, we passed cornfields on the left and soon enough Bart, Mr. Hagar's collie, bounded about us, eager to prove himself smarter than Lassie. Telling him to hush, we slipped past a bull. Whenever our father shepherded us down the lane, he made it very clear that, though tethered, this bull was no Ferdinand and that his ferocity, legendary throughout northwest Connecticut, dwarfed the minotaur's. I wonder now if we somehow transferred our fear of our father onto the bull. They had the same kind of contained power.

The Hagars' dark and fetid barn was a shock after our walk in the clear morning air. Our suburban noses took some time to adjust to the unfamiliar smells: residue of manure, milk, and the warm breath of the cows. Each of them had a name, and we were introduced. The gentlest we touched and, to the farmer's amusement, attempted to milk. The rubbery teats made us giggle, and our squeezing resulted in nothing but a swish of the tail and an unimpressed moo. Thanks to Mr. Hagar's expertise, we eventually got our reward and drank the warm, creamy liquid that tasted more like the barn itself than what we thought of as milk.

Fortified, we were ready to return home. In the distance I could see our house. The sky had held onto its brightness. Filled with rain from the night before, the brook bristled at the field's end. "Last one home's a rotten egg." But our adventure wasn't over yet. For on the way back home, we would have to stop at the Longwells' house. The Longwells were our father's friends, a family that had also escaped the city to Kent. The managing editor of Life Magazine, Dan Longwell had grown up in rural Missouri and needed his time away from New York even more than my father did.

After fending off the dachshunds at the door, we went inside the house to sit before the fire and drink Mary's hot chocolate. This always improved the taste in our mouths, and Uncle Dan would say he was thankful for the chance to stop splitting wood. We watched Mary place popcorn in the popper and hold it over the flames. Dan took advantage in the interlude to tell us about the snake he had seen sunning itself on the rocks. After Mary drizzled melted butter over the popcorn, our fingers darted at their hot targets. It was better than ice cream. We were so focused that we wouldn't notice our father until his hand swept over ours. "I was wondering what was taking you so long."

When we left the Longwells, we eyed the ground for snakes. Gradually the scent of cedar from the fire sank into the musk of fall's decaying leaves. Dad had spent the previous hour raking more leaves for us to burn. We could see his breath in the still air. "Look," he said. "Here is where that skunk was run over." We were beside the bull's pasture, but any evidence of the skunk was long gone.

"Remember Mariana's song?" I asked.

"A polecat sat on the pole," my father sang, but it did not sound the same as when it came from Mariana Sands' gravelly voice. She was one of his seven cousins, and the closest person he had ever had for a sister. Mariana was an admiral's daughter (her father had been Commandant of the Naval Academy) and she claimed that when God gave her the same baritone as Bing Crosby, He had neglected teaching her to sing. Mariana loved to talk, to capture us with story instead of song, wrapping us in that voice, letting us meet our father's father, a man we only knew from photographs.

"Oh, Johnny, you know how big he was! Well, you should have heard him tell a tale on himself. My favorite was about the time he had been swimming in York Harbor. The water there was as cold as the Arctic, but he loved to go in. Just him, surrounded by children. He would float on his back the way some of us do when we reach a certain age (that's the French way of saying "old," Johnny)... Now, where was I? Yes, Uncle Eddie, your grandfather, was on the water staring up at the sky. And you know what happened? Well, I'll tell you. A little boy, just about your age, came up to him and said, 'Mr. McIlvain, can I jump off your stomach?'"

We saw Mariana most often in Grandma's apartment in New York. This is where I heard Grandma tell the Uncle Remus stories, and listened

Eddie and my grandmother on either side of his cousin Mariana Sands, her son and daughter-in-law behind them. I am not sure who the figure on the left is, possibly another cousin (I never met Mariana's husband). I love this picture of Eddie, Mariana and my grandmother; it captures their faces in the way I like to remember them.

to her read about Farmer McGregor, where she played cards with me and taught me how to win at Slapjack and poured me some chamomile tea.

The day I learned Grandma died I acted up in class badly enough to be kicked out. The headmaster, who I had been sent to see, found me in the bathroom next to his office, crying.

We had stopped for a moment, still near the pasture, though the bull was out of site.

"I miss Grandma," I said. "Was she ever here?"

"A few times," my father said. "She loved the pond. Though you made her nervous when you leaned over the edge."

That would have been in summer, the pond with its dark, still cool water, and its mysterious bottom, layered with the leaves it trapped.

The wind picked up and I was suddenly shivering. "Hey, Dave," I said. "Race you home."

For a while there was a German couple who kept the house clean and did some cooking and welcomed us when we arrived. Then they disappeared. The house was being used less and less and there was no need for their care.

In the end just our father, David, and I went to Kent. In the morning, David and I stirred first. We whispered in the dim light of our room. The heat was turned down at night and some mornings we saw soft peaks of frost on the slit windows. Our father's snores punctuated our conversation. They were reassuring in their own way. Once, tossed by a dream, I found myself awake on the hardwood floor, shivering and lost in the dark, until the sound of his sleeping signaled where I was.

David and I joked about the noises that we made. He claimed I was worse than Dad; I told him not only did he sound like a mule, but he also stank like one. After we had run out of comparisons and the sun had warmed the house enough for us to stir, we put on our wrappers and left through the already opened door. The light in the hallway protected us from the darkness. We entered our father's room on tiptoe, wishing we had remembered slippers.

Most clear was the acrid perfume of his sleep, savory in spite of itself. In the dimness I could make out only the bed he had once shared with our mother. It filled the small room. We had to make our way around it without banging into the walls to get to the other side and watch his lips flap with every exhalation. Teeth chattering, David eventually shut the window, the banging loud enough to open my father's left eye. As soon as we saw it, we shouted "good morning" and jumped on the bed to celebrate not having to be quiet anymore.

Our next stop was the kitchen. Being there always seemed like an adventure. Every other kitchen we knew was off limits to us: the domain of the cook. Here, the cook was our father and he asked us for help. We brought milk from the refrigerator and set the table, following his instructions, hearing all the while how much better the water was here than in New York for his coffee. We enjoyed being part of the hierarchy. He was the officer, and we were the enlisted men. There was a right way to do everything, an order to follow, and that order was comforting. The kitchen was a space our father felt comfortable in, and we sensed that he was the cook too, when only he and my mother had lived here.

Breakfast always began with orange juice. Frozen juices were new and the can emerged from just above the ice trays in our father's hand. After he removed the top, he handed it to me and I squeezed until the frozen pulp plopped out into the water pitcher. Then I was told to fill the container and pour the water out of it three times. While Dad percolated the coffee,

David manned the toaster. The butter was always too hard and when he forced it onto a new piece of toast our father told him to slow down. It was not a time to hurry. The day could wait on us. It was as if the southern part of my father's heritage, the part I did not know about, took over and the rush that had been his week at work and ours at school was left behind.

I was allowed to cook the bacon if I stood far enough from the stove so that the spitting fat did not reach my eyes. There was a tin can to pour the grease into. "Now I am cooking on the front burner," I announced, echoing one of our father's favorite phrases. Meanwhile David started in on the Rice Krispies that he preferred without cream (never milk in those days) and poured ketchup on them. "What are you doing?" our father asked. I turned. "Not, you," he told me, indicating David. "Your brother."

Dad cooked the scrambled eggs slowly in a cast iron pan, stirring them with a fork, describing why you had to cook the eggs slowly and keep the fork moving lazily, making sure they did not stick to the bottom. And they were delicious. Fresh from Mr. Hagar's, the eggs had arrived on the doorstep that morning. We ate silently, and because I wolfed down my food, I always finished first and had to watch my father and brother enjoy their last bites. Afterward, with no Smith to clear off the table, and no Betty to wash the dishes, we manned our dishwashing station and cleaned up.

On Saturdays, before we went into Kent to do some shopping, we washed and simonized the Desoto. It seemed an unrewarding chore, for no combination of wax and elbow grease made the car gleam like Seebee's Rolls. He had chosen the gray because it was the color of a Navy ship (my father's next car, a Ford, was the same gray—a custom paint, he boasted). Even then I knew his was not a kind of flamboyant patriotism, but a private statement about how much his volunteering to be part of the First World War had meant to him, and how frustrated he had been when he learned he could not be part of the next one. His major contribution had been surprising Admiral Halsey by arranging for the delivery of a case of Ballantine's Scotch somewhere in the Pacific. As we worked at making the Desoto less dull, its radio played music to encourage us. Gradually we convinced ourselves that our efforts had transformed it into something we were proud to drive downtown in. When our father wiped the back windshield dry, we had earned the right to take our seats and begin the procession into town.

In Kent, everyone seemed to know us. Dad had been the honorary chief of the volunteer firemen, and people asked him why he did not come up as often anymore. As he talked, I managed to slip into one of the narrow, unlit aisles of the general store. Searching for Fig Newtons, I found them behind some saltines next to the evaporated milk.

Peggy and Eddie, with Eddie in his fire-chief's uniform.

Back home, there was the barn to explore, or the pond to catch fish in; we gathered worms near the bank of the brook and tried to hook them— Dad was teacher and master guide. The worms had a habit of dropping at my feet. Once on the ground they squiggled away from my reluctant attempts to grab them. After informing me that I was being silly, and no, I could not have gloves, Dad helped me out, easily squinching up and spearing my bait. "Now, catch a little dinner for us." Occasionally, I saw a brook trout, but it rarely responded to my lure, and I was a spectator as David stole the show. Even so, we usually dined on hamburger, mashed potatoes, and Le Sueur peas, not fresh catch.

By day's end we might have placed a tin can on a fence post and, following Dad's instructions, tried to shoot it off. To my constant surprise, David succeeded considerably more often than I. And then, we might have walked along the brook to find out where it led, or played catch with a football, or raked and burned leaves—there were always leaves—or listened to a football game on the radio. I remember Princeton, a team Dad had taken us to see a month before, crushing Yale; and Navy, winless, playing undefeated Army to a standstill. The announcer's excitement became our father's and so ours. He was back in college or back in the Navy and I was with him, my hands on the rake snagging the leaves that would escape, swooping down like a Navy defender after an errant pass.

At night he took out the steam engine. It first appeared one evening as a reward for finishing our vegetables. The bright red wheel that was attached to a stainless steel cylinder made the machine look like a miniature boiler that had been converted into a riverboat. I recall a copper wire, coiled in places and stretched out to reach the base of a lamppost. At the top of the post was a tiny bulb he assured us would light. The cylinder was filled with water, and my father struck a match and with it he touched the fuel beneath it. For some time, nothing happened. Tempted to touch it, we were not allowed to do so. Finally, wanting to give up and retire to our trains, we spotted some wisps of steam coming from the small stack amidships. The steam increased and held our attention until the wheel began to move, almost imperceptibly at first, then mounting speed until we could hear it whir, and the tiny bulb flickered like a flashlight with loose connections. Perhaps this was why I wanted to be an engineer.

Throughout, my recollection of my father in Kent was of him at his calmest. He had a temper I have inherited and he exploded at us from time to time, especially if we had done something that was risky or mindless or insensitive. I tended to associate the explosions with the city, however; with stepping out too soon to cross the street, or leaning out a window, or knocking something over, or leaving a mess that his maid Lizzie would have to pick up. Then I wanted to hide from him, as if he were the bull. Once when the doorman had greeted me warmly, only to watch me tear past him to be the first one to get to the elevator, my father told me to go back and say I was sorry for having forgotten my manners.

"Do it now," my father said.

"Now?"

"Now," my father said again. "Raymond works hard so that everyone in this building will feel at home. I respect him and you must, too."

"Now?"

"*Now.*"

We were afraid when he raised his voice. It came upon us suddenly and we were momentarily frozen. I apologized to Raymond.

There must have been moments at Kent, too, when he flashed disapproval.

"Don't," he said once, "ever point a gun at your brother."

"But Dad, it's a cap pistol."

"Don't."

"But…" I felt silent, afraid of being gored. My brothers looked pleased.

"You are the oldest," he said.

But I can remember no specific incidents at Kent when I might have trembled in fear. Perhaps I have suppressed them, just as I hide from some of the prejudices he held. He always embraced individuals on their own terms, even when they were part of a race or religion he would at times disparage. He thought people should be admired not for what they did but for how well they did it. Mr. Hagar was every bit as good a man as he himself was. A missing tooth made him no less of a person. He could teach us more about life than most of the teachers he had ever known. And Dan Longwell, whose father was a farmer, was worth twenty of almost any man he knew.

In time, our trips to Kent were spread further and further apart. When my brother Eddie was old enough to go along, he and David used to battle every mile of the trip. Once, the car door flew open and a hat landed on Route 7. Dad was ready to murder them, and the Desoto ready to die for the cause.

It was winter when we said good-bye to Kent each year. Snow covered the ground, and the house, heatless, was locked. We looked through the windows and saw the braided rugs and pine furniture hidden in the shadows of the low-ceilinged living room. Our father told us to go skating, but first we fogged the windows and wrote our names on the panes with gloved fingers.

We yelled back from the pond that we needed a shovel to clear the ice, and Dad—we always called him Dad or Daddy whereas our mother was always "Mother"—shouted back that he

My father shoveling snow in Kent.

would bring one up when he came. I watched him walk toward the garage. It was cold. I wanted to be near a fire. The sky seemed low and forbidding as if it was overhanging the mountain, a roof that would fall down if the wind, so large and loud, blew any harder. The sun, a pale, shrunken copy of its summer self, appeared as an impotent spectator, gazing coolly at the lifeless earth. Nothing moved anywhere except the menacing branches of the trees. I thought of the few remaining leaves and felt secure in my heavy clothes.

Our footsteps had created a crease in the snowfield, and Dad, carrying the shovel, deepened it. He moved slowly, careful not to fall as David and I had in our earlier scramble. "Here you go!" he called out, and we realized we were expected to meet him halfway. Off we went, charging at him and clamoring, "Give it to me! Give it to me!"

The snow on the ice was only a few inches deep, and I quickly made the rink, a narrow corridor of about thirty feet. We had brought hockey sticks and a puck and would be the Rangers and the Red Wings. The ice was ribbed like corduroy, but our skates were galoshes so the surface didn't bother us.

"Let's warm up!" I said.

"How?"

"By taking shots."

"O.K."

"I'll go first."

I took a mighty swipe but fanned and fell on all fours. David laughed so hard he almost fell himself and was still sneering when I made my second swipe. I had eased up to make sure of contact and the puck dribbled his way.

"Save!" he boasted. David would go on to star as the goalie on the Hill School hockey team. "Now it's my turn."

"Not that way!" I said when he held his stick like a baseball bat.

Whap! He had ignored me and swung before I was ready. The puck skittered by me and hopped off the rink.

"Rah! Rah! Rah!" David cheered.

Not responding to the taunt, I headed toward where I thought the puck had landed.

"It didn't go that far."

"It could have. It could have skidded along here where the snow has blown off."

"I don't think so."

"Well, I do,' I announced triumphantly, "and I see it."

The puck had gone even farther than I had thought and lay about twenty feet beyond me, near the end of the pond where the water that had been diverted from the brook ran out to rejoin it.

"Careful," David said.

"What for? I won't fall. Look..."

I proved my point by running a few steps and then gliding over the bumpy surface. My arms whirled to maintain my balance. Pleased at my feat, I repeated it and reclaimed the puck, proclaiming greatness. In one motion I picked it off the ice and tossed it to David.

"My shot," I said, just before I heard the cracking. The ice gasped and I sank, flailing, into the water.

"Dad! Dad! Dad! Dad!"

I heard David's alarm as I grabbed for the closest ice. It held, but when I tried to pull myself onto it, it broke off in my hands, crumbling like the crusted sand on Singing Beach. David began flapping his arms and shouting, "Hurry!"

For a moment, I wondered if he were afraid that one of the leviathans that lived in the pond would eat my legs. In the summer we hated to swim in the pond because of the trout that nibbled at our bait and the mucky bottom. I thrashed a little more, supposing I could hurl myself from the numbing water like a flying fish.

Clearing the pond at Kent. In summer, the water level was near the top
of the wall.

"Dad's coming," David promised. The words relaxed me some, enough
so I stopped my frenzied motions. I wasn't a fish, but in a minute all would
be well. I gripped the ice as if it were the side of our pool in Long Island.
I looked around. David had rushed off the pond. All I could see were the
abandoned hockey sticks and the puck. Above and beyond them, shad-
owy and still belonging to the Indians, rose the bleak and unsympathetic
mountain.

"The stick," my father said, from somewhere. "Give him the stick."

"But I'll fall, too."

David was edging toward me.

"Do what I say. Give me the other stick. Now, I'll pull you, and you
pull Johnny. Hold on tight. Johnny, grab the stick with one hand and use
the other to lift yourself."

I did as I was told. The ice held and I slid forward onto the surface of the pond.

"Get up," my father ordered, "and run back to the house!"

But I was afraid to move. When I did, the water sloshed in my boots. I slipped to the ice. David helped me up. "Bring him here," my father said. When I reached him, he told me he wasn't angry and to lean on him. Nothing bad would happen to me; he would help me walk.

I changed, shivering, in an open courtyard that was sheltered by a corner of the house. The sun was higher now and less ashen. All around me I could hear the plop of water from the melting icicles hitting the wet stones. I was chattering now, comparing my adventures to the Pilgrims. Someone found me dry clothes from my suitcase, and I put them on while my father draped his overcoat around me. Teeth chattering, I said I couldn't wait to tell everything to the Longwells. They had moved out of the valley to a house high above the Housatonic, and we were going to have lunch with them that day. Rattling on, I was hustled into the DeSoto, its engine already running, its heater on high. I looked at the house. It seemed to grow out of the snow, its small second story windows the squinty eyes of a gigantic snowman. The only color anywhere was the green of the shutters. We left quickly and did not look back.

I have a watercolor that someone gave my father. It is dated July 4, 1949, his fifty-third birthday, two summers before my icy adventure. The picture shows a rambling white house surrounded by lawn and trees. The mountain I remember has dissolved in the face of a sun-brightened sky. Roses climb all the way up to where icicles glistened. The painting itself strikes me as naïve, as if painted by an adult pretending to be a child. It seems to be saying that it will be summer forever. The leaves won't turn, and the snow won't fall. If it does, I will get a paperwhite to grow beside my deck. Somehow it will remind me of Kent. I will be ten again and if anything goes wrong, my father and brother will reappear to rescue me.

Our mother Peggy with Eddie on her lap, and David and me on either side, featuring Froofroo, beneath her portrait that spent most of the following years in a basement. This must have been shortly before our parents divorced as it looks to have been taken in our New York apartment.

BROTHERS

"Hey!"

"What?"

"You know what."

"No. What?"

"I'm not going to tell you."

"Come on."

"You won't believe it."

"So?"

"Are you ready?"

"Of course, I'm ready."

"Well then, you're in for a shock."

"What is it?"

"Well, I'm not your real brother."

"How come?"

"I'm adopted."

"Sure."

"I am."

"I don't believe it."

"See, I knew you wouldn't."

"Prove it."

The best thing about my family is that we all seem to get along. I attribute this at least in part to my mother's influence. At the end of the sixties, she seemed to have little trouble with my shoulder length hair or my brother Miguel's devotion to the Grateful Dead. She once suggested it might be nice to have a marijuana party so that the young could relax. Where her tolerance and lack of an insistence on certain protocols came from is unclear. Although my second stepfather, George, to whom she was married for almost fifty years, was a lover of protocol, he also loved her enough to allow his inclination to disapprove of our antics to surface as a kind of puzzled bemusement. I am not sure my father could have been so restrained.

Whatever the reason for siblings to unite, my brothers, my sister Sydney, and I have always enjoyed each other's company without reservation. Sometimes I like to think our missing brother Eddie, who was killed in Vietnam, still draws us together. The four of us have all ended up leading different lives, but these differences have never interfered with our affection. When David, Miguel, and Sydney emerged one after the other out of Miguel's car to celebrate my seventieth birthday at my home in Maine, I loved how pleased they looked to have surprised me. We like each other. We like having family reunions. We like each other's children. Our children like each other.

That David and I feel this way makes a certain amount of sense because we were so close growing up. We felt that intimacy with Eddie, too. But I was twelve when Miguel was born and seventeen when Sydney was born. They grew up in circumstances similar to mine, almost strangers in our own home, though Miss Wilcox, the last m'am'selle, was a steadier presence for Miguel and Sydney than any in David, Eddie, and my potpourri of m'am'selles.

On the other hand, David and I had each other and we had Eddie, and each of us was antidote to the other's emptiness.

"Why don't you ask me who my real father is?"

"Because you'll tell me, and anyway I know."

"Who then?"

"My real father is Hoot Gibson."

"The cowboy?"

"No, the baseball player."

"Oh, of course. He'd be on the Tigers."

"He let me be adopted because he had to travel all the time. But I get to see him twice a year."

"That's the dumbest thing I ever heard."

"But it's true."

"I'll ask Mother."

"She won't tell you."

"Why not?"

"Because she's not supposed to. I only found out by accident."

"What accident?"

"I saw a letter on her desk."

"Oh. But you said you see him twice a year."

"I do."

"Well, when did you find out by reading the letter?"

"A few years ago."

"You are a liar. Such a liar."

"Say what you want. It's true."

"If he's your father, who's your mother?"

"A nice lady from Detroit."

"Probably one of Seebee's maids."

"So what if it was?"

"This is stupid."

"What's stupid?"

"I'm not talking anymore. I want to go to sleep."

"What's the matter? Tired?"

"I'm not talking to you anymore."

"I bet I can get you to…. Moomoo Moose made faces at you on the bus today. I think she wanted to kiss you on the lips."

"That's what you wanted."

"See, David, I knew you were only pretending to sleep."

"Mmm…"

I am somewhere between the age of eight and twelve—most likely, judging by the conversation, I am closer to eight than twelve—still, years later, when we have moved to Wynnewood outside of Philadelphia, our conversations continue fending off the threat of loneliness. Our words, our voices, formed a tent against the night. But we were in Long Island then, sharing the room in which we assaulted Miss Broadfoot. That was sometime after M'am'selle Van Snyck was released for celebrating our nakedness. Our home was a classy Georgian estate Seebee gave to my mother after she married John Braganza, an event that must have happened simultaneously with the divorce from my father. One day we had been in the New York apartment, then we had our weeks in Grosse Pointe, then we were in Long Island. John Braganza might have been my mother's second husband, but John was descended from royalty and had a royal name, and no doubt my grandmother took pride in this. She would not have wanted the fact that the newlyweds had no money to hurt their standing.

The house was neither as formal nor as grand as Seebee's home in Grosse Pointe, but it was splendid in its own right, tasteful with its white-washed brick, and beautifully situated above Beaver Dam in Mill Neck, an enclave of estates on Long Island's north shore where a policeman (Officer Casey) cruised down driveways after midnight to check for interlopers. Today, it looks as impressive as ever from Beaver Dam, the skating club down below it. A student of mine, a friend of my daughter's who knew our perfectly comfortable house in Huntington, looked up at it once and asked, "Mr. Mac, I know there's nothing wrong with where you live now, but really, what happened?"

David with Mischief.

The basement in the house was a catacomb of gloomy rooms to which David, Eddie, and I were exiled on rainy days. We did not mind and frequently looked forward to the chance to bury ourselves down there, away from M'am'selle and from sounds of vacuums and of buffers polishing the waxed floors above us. If it was a kind of a minimum-security prison, it was also the indoor place where we had the most freedom. Even on a perfectly cloudless summer day—one that began with our version of the Olympics, and moved on to baseball and getting our dog Mischief to find the ball I had just let fly into the tall grass—we headed toward the basement. Tired from running, we needed a retreat from the sun when it became too hot for us, and when the pool was being refilled as it was every Wednesday with frigid water we were told was from Connecticut.

In the basement it was possible to lie back and do nothing in the dank coolness for a while. Looking at the stippled plaster ceiling was easier than trying to pick up a fly ball in the sun. Only our secret hideouts in the woods were more protective than the basement,

and some days they seemed too distant to reach, and it made more sense to slip inside and carry out our dreams. These dreams were a byproduct of the cowboy films that filled the nine-inch screen of our television set; we lived in black and white, good and evil, with Hopalong Cassidy and Tex Ritter, Cochise and Geronimo. We drifted from Laredo to Tombstone, danger in every inch of the sagebrush, always armed.

"Kkkhhew!" A bullet whizzed by my ear. Quickly, I was up, scrambling off the musty sofa out of the room and into the unlit hall.

"Where'd he go?" Eddie asked David. The room was dark, part of the rules.

"Over there... *kkkhhew!*"

"I think he's gone outside."

"Or to the bathroom."

"Maybe he's not playing."

"It's just a trick."

"Kkkhhew!"

"What are you shooting at?"

"Nothing."

"Oh."

I remain in hiding. I know if I am still long enough they will lose focus and begin to argue. Patience will gain me the advantage.

"Kkkhhew!"

"Stop shooting."

"Why?"

"You'll run out of bullets."

"That's dumb."

"No, it isn't."

"Yes, it is. You think you know everything."

"Well, I know more than you do."

"Since when?"

"What's the capital of Wisconsin?"

"That's dumb."

"No, it's Madison."

"Who cares?"

"It shows I'm smarter."

"No, it doesn't."

"Yes, it does."

"Want to bet?"

"How much?"

I could make them out in the far corner of the room. I had snuck through a passageway—once a bar, now used for stealth missions—to a second door. I enjoyed listening to their squabbling. Sometimes I saw myself as above the fray, and I would engineer conflict between them and then look to the nearest adult to indicate how I was past such childishness. Today I had a different plan.

"*Kkkhhew!... Kkkhhew!...* Got you! Got you both," I shouted in triumph.

But I was too late, for David and Eddie were already on the floor, attacking me with all they had. My bullets had bounced off both of them, my victory unnoticed.

"Come on, you guys, cut it out..."

I was ignored. I was annoyed. They were not following the rules. Mine, not theirs. "Your rules are stupid." Mayhem followed.

"No fair pulling hair."

"Well, you bit me."

"I did not."

"Yes, you did, and I'll bite you back."

"No, you won't."

"Arrrggh!"

"Ouch. Aiyeeee!! Kill!"

"David, no biting."

"Who asked you?"

One of the pillows that belonged to the sofa lay at my feet. It had been used earlier as a shield when the idea was to get me. I picked it up and transformed it into a mace. After raising it above my head, I whirled it around and then brought it down, trying to cleave my brothers the way Paul Bunyan would a tree stump. For a second they froze, unimpressed, but surprised, torn between avenging themselves on me or on one another. I whacked at them again, accompanying the blow with a cry worthy of a Cheyenne brave. This time they divided and scrambled for a weapon.

Whole nations disappeared. At the front enough blood is spilled to stain Little Big Horn. No matter, we kept on coming. Eyes shut to protect against dust, we struck blindly, no idea who would be victim to our thunderous thwops. There were no time outs. The hits accelerated, careening in from all sides. Our arms had become our pillows and our pillows were yanking us around to where they wanted to land. There could be no escape. The couch came out of the dimness sporadically and was apt to look upside down. Any momentary lull was quickly obliterated with shouts of, "Die! Die!" and a fresh onslaught began.

The madness ended abruptly. A voice from above announced, "Suppertime!" The truce arranged, the light switch was turned on, and we tucked in our shirts and saw the battlefield transformed into just an extension of our messy rooms. We had no time to pick it up. Who cared? The chances were that a few days would pass before anyone came down to see how bad it was. The basement had become a ghost town to all but us. The people who had lived here before had used it all the time, as if the more formal rooms above it were only for display. Our domain included a bathroom and, off a corridor long enough to have spring training catches, changing rooms for the pool. Small dances had been held where we'd gone into battle, and women's heels had pocked the maroon floor long before it took our bullets.

We were not always armed. After supper, we'd return to the basement and watch that nine-inch screen nine inches from the eyes m'am'selles warned us would soon go blind. Captain Video would take us off to the Sea of Tranquility where we would stay until one of us wanted a different program, and then it was back to war again.

The greatest winners in the history of sports were not the Yankees. They were the Mill Neck Devils and the Mill Neck Yellow Jackets. And their prowess was hardly limited to one sport, nor their stars to one season. The Red and White, the Yellow and Black—they won at basketball as well as baseball, at hockey as well as football. Fortunately these two juggernauts arranged never to meet each other. With so many All-Americans going after each other, the fans might have gone wild and torn down the stadium.

The games, a kind of primitive and rigged prequel to fantasy sports, were usually played with cards and stretched out for hours on winter weekend afternoons. Every yard gained, every homerun hit was recorded for posterity in composition books as if putting our fantasy on paper made it more substantial. Taking one of the books off the shelf would allow us to step instantly into this secret, adult-free other place.

Our Wonderland was limited to the familiar. David and I played by the rules of the games. Our line-ups were not filled with imaginary creatures, but with the names of friends, destined to become legends without ever knowing it (probably just as well as none of them quite measured up to the inventors of the game itself). We would score more touchdowns in the course of a February weekend spent in our room than Red Grange had in all his years on the gridiron.

Sometimes the secret lay in cheating. In any form of solitaire, the dealer has a certain amount of discretionary power. Fate could be overlooked, distorted, or defied. New rules could suddenly emerge to make the best of a difficult situation. The two of diamonds that had been a strike out just a minute before could become a double when I stepped to the plate. There was no way that either one of our teams was about to lose. Still, the thrill of victory was diminished when it had more to do with the manager than the team. The best games were always those that needed no interference—the ones won because the cards had arranged themselves in the home team's favor. There were glorious days when the aces always seemed to fall at the right time, inning after inning, quarter after quarter. Opponents were routed because chance had lined up against them.

If I thought I could win a game of solitaire, I would play one right now. I would pick up the deck and talk to the cards again, trying to convince them to work for me. I remember spending half a summer avoiding writing by giving myself over to the mystery of the cards, cheering them on when they seemed moved by my will. The right color queen would appear, and I would feel elated, as if she were Cinderella's godmother come to rescue me from a world where coping was essential for survival.

In the end I have not become an addict, either to solitaire or cards or gambling in any form. I am in no fantasy leagues. I still am a true sports fan, especially baseball and football, but they are no obsession. It is as if the hours I spent on my own and with my brother satisfied my need once and forever. We had invented our own imitation of some great American pastimes in order to pass the hours when we had nothing else to do. We played in our hot-stove leagues and kept meticulous records. There were few other distractions available, no television programs, no iPads, no Internet.

Occasionally a child-turned-sportscaster (more Mel Allen than Red Barber) would interrupt the automated rhythm of the cards. "And how about that, sports fans, that ball is going, going, it is gone... another four bagger for Bob Kellogg, his sixteenth of the season. How about that!"

"Sure," I said, getting up to check that it had really happened.

"See," David said, showing me the four of clubs.

"I believe you," I said, and looked up. "Hey, it's snowing," I said, but David was too busy to look. The paperwork took longer than the plays.

I went to the window. The snow had been falling for a while and the ground, which I remembered as being muddy and unwelcoming, was now white and swirling.

"Maybe we can sled tomorrow."

David wasn't listening. He was flipping some more cards, watching his team run the bases under the sunshine of a bedside lamp. My players weren't faring quite as well. Some had slipped onto the floor when I had gotten up. The manager was furious and gave them a tongue-lashing.

"I'm quitting."

"Not me," David said. "This is my best game."

"Come on, " I said. "Let's do something."

"Like what?"

"I don't know. Anything. We could ride our bikes and make tracks."

"I don't want to go outside. It's too cold."

"How about Eddie? Maybe we could do something with him. He must be up now."

"We're not supposed to play with him, remember? He's being punished for the pen he stole."

"Oh," I said, glad that David had already returned to his seven run eighth. I would not interrupt again. Instead I went into the bathroom and examined myself in the mirror. All the freckles had remained in place. The hazel eyes had not changed color. Cowardice was invisible. Crime had paid.

Eddie. He would survive the accusation. He was good at being a victim, for punishment always seemed to strengthen his stubborn spirit. As for me, already I had managed to forget for an hour that I was a liar and a thief. My plan was to wait my conscience out, to let it slacken over time. I would do nothing to stir the embers, and the scar would heal nicely. If, by chance, the flames flared, by then I would be either annealed or altered enough to be burned without pain. After all, I had only meant to borrow the pen and would have confessed as much if I had not been so afraid. But I had not counted on someone else being blamed.

Back on my bed, I picked up the cards and shuffled them. It would be best to start up a new game. Top of the first. Devils vs. Garden City.

"Batter up!" I said.

David was the athlete. Lithe and graceful, he won tournaments and prizes all the time. He was even able to catch more fish than I did whenever we went on spring excursions with our father. They were out of the inlet in Boynton Beach, after we had been roused at dawn for the half hour drive from my grandmother's house in Palm Beach, in hopes we would return with a worthwhile catch.

Sometimes the bobbing of the boat made me seasick and I sought refuge below decks, leaving the glory to my brother. Lying on a bunk, I could hear the sudden whirring of a line, and the engine changing speeds. A voice followed, shouting advice, "Let her off a bit... reel it in... hard!" I'd close my eyes, hoping that sleep might put me on ice until we docked, where other salts would saunter over and judge our catch. But that was hours off, and the brightness of the sun ensured there would be no shortcuts in reaching it. I had to be satisfied with staring at the huge hooks swinging near my head. It was dumb to get seasick; it was time to get back into the air, to sit in the chair, check the line and catch something.

I daydreamed about beating David in tennis. It was still possible, although it would not be for long. My power would soon succumb to his coordination, my temper to his patience. Terrifying him with screams and threats, insulting the softness of his shots, questioning the accuracy of his calls—all this in time would prove futile. I was crushing overheads, winning love and love, and nearing the finals at Forest Hills. At the end I leapt the net, and the cheers of thousands drowned out the droning, flattened the chop, took the bonito back into the sea. The spell held for a treasured second, teetered, fell into the persistent reality of the boat's cabin, the smell of the bait, the restless horizon, the relentless dull roar reestablishing its dominion.

"Score?"

"Thirty-love."

"Are you sure?"

"Yeah, you hit the first one over the line, remember?"

He served, gently as always, and I cracked a forehand into the net. My racket followed.

"This is the worst," I announced, "the worst I have ever played."

David ignored me as he often did in such situations. Placid and unresponsive, he awaited my recovery. Earlier, when I had been ahead, he had paid little attention to my antics. I had babbled on this and that placement like a parrot to its echo. Now, I pictured my mother telling me for the two thousandth time that his temperament was something I should try to copy.

She would never order him and his bag off the golf course for throwing his club toward a tree. No. That was always me.

But I was not about to copy Mr. Wonderful. "Let's take a break," I said.

"A break?" he said.

"A break. It's too hot. I need a coke."

"The machine doesn't work," he said. "Anyhow, I think we should keep playing."

"Nope," I said, and walked off the court.

"I win," he said.

"Come on," I said. "I just want a drink. You can wait for me. There's nothing wrong with having a coke."

"I don't know," he said, but couldn't find the words to keep arguing and began to follow me.

"Are you coming, too?"

"Why? Aren't I allowed to?"

"Of course you are," I said, no longer his opponent but a trusted guide, leading Natty Bumpo through the forest to a sweet water spring. We had to traipse through some woods to get from the dusty clay courts to the oasis by the eleventh green, where drinks were served with cocktail napkins, and port wine cheese could be spread on small round crackers.

We were playing in a tournament at Piping Rock, our home away from home for parts of the summer when I was twelve or thereabouts. Piping was a club where the generations rarely crossed, where parents bridged and golfed and played tennis on grass, and their children were located in the part of the club that was down and to the right as you drove in, and which featured clay courts red as Roland Garros. Sometimes supervised and sometimes ignored, when no one was in charge, we could cross the line from our demesne to theirs. On stifling summer days, we became seditious, desperate enough to sign a chit and sip lemonade slowly under the suspicious frown of a legendary fogey.

It was a tournament I would go on to win, beating the favorite rather easily the next day. The break gave me the time to recover and win the match against David, though I knew even then it was a hollow victory, not really a victory at all. I was incapable of allowing my brother to beat me and had done whatever it took not to lose. My temper was monumental. It was almost entirely self-directed. I broke my rackets (wood in those days) in almost every way imaginable: the short chop, the long fling, the baseball swing against a metal post. I hated to lose.

Over time I tempered my rage. In my thirties, when I played competitive squash, I was expressive but a good sport. People today who didn't know me when I was young are surprised when I tell them about my outbursts. I hide my temper well most of the time. Now, it tends to surface over lost keys. I have had road rage only once and it was nothing compared to the guy whose car I bumped.

"John?"

"Yes."

"Remember the tournament you won at Piping Rock?"

"Not really." I was lying. "That was so long ago. I remember before I played that guy, I sat on a bee in the changing room at the beach. I think that's why I won. I was too sore to be nervous."

"Remember the match before? The one you cheated in?"

"Cheated? I don't remember that." I lied a second time.

"When I was ahead. And you made me leave the court. And when we finally came back you made me start the third set over again?"

"Are you sure?"

"Positive.

"Well, I don't remember."

"Jake does."

"Jake?"

"Jake."

"Jake wants to talk to you. Jake wants to kiss you on the lips good night. He thinks it will help you remember."

"Get away."

"Just a little kiss on the lips."

"Away."

I was too afraid to move. It was a moonless night, one so dark I could barely make out where the window was. I wanted to go for the light switch but was sure Jake would be guarding it, ready to nip my hands and cause the bones to run out, leaving my fingers looking like so many discarded snake skins.

Jake had come after Long Island, when we had moved again, this time to Wynnewood on the Main Line outside Philadelphia. Jake was a gift to David from George, our new stepfather, who had picked him up on a post-war adventure in Ecuador. At first I had not been concerned. If my brother enjoyed the company of a shrunken head, that was his problem. I spent most of my time in boarding school. Why should I lose sleep over the withered face with a wart on its left cheek and the slight beard that David had taken to stroking?

"Jake remembers," David hissed in Jake's menacing voice.

"Well, that's his problem. I don't care." A nonchalant reply.

"Don't you? Jake doesn't like that too much. Do you, Jake?"

"David, let's go to sleep."

"Jake is wandering tonight. He wants to pay you a visit."

"David, no! David! I remember! I promise I remember."

I shouted out my confession and listened for an acknowledgment. But my brother's voice had disappeared. The loud music of a Pennsylvania summer night rang in my ears. Jake was on the move. His yellow teeth were near my toes. I jerked my foot away.

"Whoooooooooooooo. Jake is going to chase you through the night. Whooooooooooo."

"David, cut it out."

"Cut what out? Your head. Ha, ha, ha, ha. Whoooooooooo."

David's howl diffused into the chirruping of the crickets, and I prayed for school to start, prayed I was back there and the buzzer was going to ring any second, waking me, leaving me to yawn and stretch in the darkness of a midwinter morning. I would dress in my warmest clothes and run over to a breakfast of hot oatmeal and my bleary companions quizzing each other in Latin.

"AAAAAAAAAAAAAGGGGHHH!!!"

"Jesus Christ, David. Now I'm mad."

"At poor little Jakey."

"If I catch him, I'm going to throw him out the window."

"Not if you're afraid to touch him."

"I can do it just once. I'll get gloves."

"He'll come back to haunt you. He'll curse you forever."

"I don't care."

"Poor little Jakey-kins."

With that I lunged for the light and twisted the switch on. The room was the same as always, sloped ceilings (we were on the third floor) and greenish wallpaper. Our bureaus were still in place at the ends of the room. Our clothes were scattered about randomly. David was smiling, the shrunken head propped on his pillow.

"Promise you won't do that anymore," I said.

"Tonight?"

"Tonight."

"Okay," he said cheerfully, and placed Jake on top of the chair on the side of his bed that was away from mine.

"Good night," I said.

"Good night."

My heart quieted and the returning darkness seemed friendlier. The crickets continued to sing in their insistent rhythm. I tried to hear David's breathing over it, but couldn't and wondered if he were listening for mine. I could pretend to be asleep and that might help us both relax our vigil. I began to inhale and exhale ponderously and thought of the fish we used to catch displayed and gasping on the pier beside the chartered boat. There was a group picture taken of us, our sunburned faces, arms and legs almost vermillion beside our pale booty. The sudden roar of a diesel engine was enough to disperse the crickets. We were at sea again, the captain on the tuna tower looking for marlin, the hooks swinging silently over a dreaming boy.

I would finally exorcize Jake on a skiing vacation in Aspen when I threw him out the second story window of Floradora Cottage into the snow. Feeling guilty and perhaps afraid that Jake could muster some terrifying vengeance, I would help my outraged brother to rescue him. We braved our fear that a dog in the neighborhood might beat us to him and the greater fear that the dog would use Jake as a decoy and turn on us. Our mission was a success, thanks to a flashlight and the moon, and we returned Jake indoors. But he was never the same after that. His spell had been broken. He had embodied all of my fears of the unknown, the lion in the chair, the alligator under the bed, the cold flesh of the fish that David caught more frequently than I—all that was alien to me. Jake had provided David the chance to pay me back years of having to endure the way I punished him for being something other than my shadow. I have suppressed whatever payments I had exacted along the way, but he was not going to let me forget that I had cheated him out of that tennis match.

I'm not sure what happened to Jake, where he went after I had sent him into the winter night. Perhaps we didn't find him and my memory is playing tricks. Perhaps David continued to use him to torment me, but I don't think so. I think he knew if I had done it once I could do it again. We were even.

I remember an Indian summer day one October. I had no soft pretzels to chew, no mustard to spill on my clothes, no pennants to wave, no pins with tigers or gold footballs dangling from them. I had my heart, if anything, beat faster, and my cheers, if anything, were louder. Instead of coming in on a train from New York, in a special car full of whisky and my father's Princeton '18 friends, I had driven alone. Instead of climbing to our seats halfway up Palmer Stadium, I was pacing on a sideline in the middle of nowhere, or to be more precise in New Lebanon, New York. I had not come to see Kazmaier, but Eddie, play football. The week before he had run and returned for 400 yards, something ridiculous like that, and his team was undefeated. I thought about how much our father would have liked to watch this, for not only was his youngest son a captain and the star, but also the Darrow School's uniforms were Princeton's orange and black (they might have actually been Princeton uniforms, because their own had been burned in a fire), and its team ran the single wing.

They used a nine-man line to stop Eddie's running, so he passed instead. He was no Y.A. Tuttle, but he was good enough to throw for a couple of touchdowns that set up the pair he ran for later. The coach told me it was not one of his better performances, that the heat had slowed him down some. Still it was a long way from my own attempts to star from the bench. He played as I had only dreamed of playing. I was the brother who had left my cleats back in the locker room, the motionless son in uniform and black tie shoes whose poor father never saw play. At least later, our father had the chance to cheer for a son when David was the quarterback for Hill School.

Eddie was a big (200 pounds was big in those days), hard-hitting back, faster than those he was up against and a little meaner, too. In our games he was always the center, hiking it to David or me so we could run or pass as we chose. If he was lucky, he might get to catch a pass or take a lateral on the last play before dinner. Otherwise, he was relegated to setting up for the next play.

Somewhere, though, he had slipped past us. So much so that in our last brother footrace, David and I tried to beat him as a relay team and didn't come close. He stood over our hunched and humiliated forms cheering himself for his victory and we could only laugh. We had dreamed enough, but he had worked hard so it did not matter that David could throw the ball farther, or that I could catch it a little more surely. He had picked it off in midair and flown away with it. He had become what my ten-year-old self, that star of the Mill Neck Devils, had dreamed I'd be.

Three years later Eddie would write us from Vietnam.

For an instant I must have been frozen because I remember having to tell myself to move before I heard any shots. I had to cross a kind of field to where our injured were. They'd dropped me about a hundred yards off from them and it took me a second to orient myself, to know I was where I was, to know that all the training I had had for the past year was to prepare me for this moment in the middle of nowhere. I started toward the men before the first shots came and I was running as I had been taught, low and zigzagging, but nothing seemed especially out of the ordinary until the shots came. It was the shots that made it not a dream and even then it took me a few steps before I understood that someone was actually trying to kill me, a thought that registered and struck me as strange. I remember feeling that even as I started running faster and more evasively. It was football all over again, I felt that, and felt confident that I was going to make it to our men as soon as I pictured myself running through a broken secondary. So it all made a kind of weird sense to me.

The boys minus fathers, just after Miguel was born.

We all have our leave-takings. One of mine came some fourteen years before that letter, back in Mill Neck, less than a month after my twelfth birthday, right after Miguel was born.

"Hey, Dave?"

"What?"

"Keep in touch."

"Oh, sure."

"No, I mean it."

"Are you scared?"

"A little."

"Me, too. I wish you weren't going."

"Same here, but I guess I have to."

"Why?"

"I don't know, I just do. You know how that kind of thing is."

"Well, you'll get a new room when you get back."

"I like that."

"I get to room with Eddie."

"Good luck.

"And Miguel gets Eddie's room."

"You did a good job this afternoon."

"When you were pitching good curves."

"We've got to get someone else to bat. Eddie's too small."

"Well, maybe next year."

I was twelve and trying not to be upset about leaving for boarding school. After all, I had been away before—to camp twice—and so it was not going to be a completely new experience. I held my pillow, thinking of the Teddy I had left on a train years before, thinking of Mischief and the baseball he'd found that afternoon, thinking of all the Devils games left in the drawer, thinking of the birthday I had had when I had met Joe DiMaggio—but thinking mostly of David and Eddie and the basement sanctuary I was leaving behind. We would have a final finger-football game. I promised David that before I went to sleep.

Miss Wilcox, Peggy, John Braganza, David and Eddie bid me farewell.

The Chapel at Brooks.

SCHOOL

Two days later I woke up on a metal bed in a cubicle in boarding school. Coming after three years at St. Bernard's in New York and four at Greenvale on Long Island, and before a month-long stint at Lower Merion High School and a semi-repeat senior year at Garland (a school that embraced godsons of Trujillo and others difficult to place), Brooks School in Massachusetts was my third school of five. To me the others barely count. When, after five and a half years, I was expelled for having slipped into the neighboring city of Lawrence to go to the movies, it was as if half of my life had been stripped from me.

The day I arrived I was a young twelve and also essentially parentless. The school became the last of my m'am'selles, the ultimate surrogate. The institution must have known its role as my situation was hardly unique, but it was modeled on the British public school (by way of Groton) and had confidence that in the end its boys would benefit from the mixture of tradition, hazing, and chapel that such schools celebrate. I did not. To Brooks I was someone who never seemed to  live up to his potential. And they were right, although neither they nor I had the slightest idea as to why.

The daffodils were out, emerging bright and brave through the overgrown and tattered ivy. Pansies had been planted along the chapel walk. I was one of the youngest of the school's one hundred and seventy boys—

there were no girls then—and I bent down to pick a blossom, one with yellow-fringed petals surrounding a dark brown face, and placed it in the buttonhole of my navy blazer. Several of the boys walking near me did the same thing, and a woman, standing to the side, smiled in approval.

Inside, I went to my knees to pray. It was difficult to concentrate and I stared at my hands for inspiration. All I could think of was how soft the petals of the flower were. They grazed my cheek and assured me their touch was deeper than any message I might come up with for God. So I left my knees and sat back in the wooden pew.

The chapel itself was neither intimidating nor ostentatious. The school was ostensibly non-denominational, as the simplicity of this building showed with its white walls and clear glass windows. The services, though, were low-church Episcopalian, rooted in *The Book of Common Prayer* and the same as those at St. John's of Lattingtown, our church on Long Island. There I had won a softball for being the most improved boy in my Sunday school class the year before, an honor for which my brothers had mocked me, but that had inspired me to choose a lurid and glittery crucified Jesus for my prize at a Coney Island ring toss. Here, I was determined to build upon my early flashes of devotion.

After dinner was Evening Prayer. Every Sunday was Morning Prayer. All the visiting preachers were Episcopalian; they appeared once a month to perform the Eucharist. I was not confirmed, but I had taken communion several times, and I colored thinking about it, aware that I was not supposed to taste the bread and wine but not sure, now that I had, how I could forsake it. At the time it seemed the natural thing to do, a way to show that I was not completely frivolous. It had never occurred to me that it, too, would need exculpation.

The first formers (seventh graders to the rest of the country) sat together across from the choir. The youngest class in the school, we waited restlessly for the headmaster to appear. He emerged from a door directly across from us and then crossed in front of us to his kneeler, upon which he spent thirty seconds. When he left it to sit back in his chair, there was no question that in the minds of his youngest audience he had left the world of the senses behind. He and God had exchanged more than the time of day.

Despite this, even while the headmaster was praying, even after he was sitting silent in contemplation, the laughter of some of the more dilatory seniors could be heard over the solemnity of the prelude. They were still outside, resisting until the last minute the entreaties of the tight-lipped masters who wanted them to hurry in and make less joyful sounds.

Mike Keating had just handed me a note, but I sensed I was being observed and left it unopened in my hand. The last thing I needed was for some bored prefect to come swooping down from behind and signal that after chapel retribution would take up the free time until study hall. My humiliation would provide entertainment for the elders. No matter what it contained, the note was not worth looking at. No, not even if it was a caricature of John Ross. One glance at the Semitic nose and the mole with the three crooked hairs next to it that worked their way across the cheek— one glance would have been all that was needed to bring on the snort of suppressed hilarity and the concomitant punishment.

The last first form in the history of Brooks School. I am on the bottom row left. I believe only two of us graduated.

Everyone rose to sing the hymn. It was an Easter hymn and the celebration continued. Alleluias resounded. I was dueling the note passer and our voices floated above the rest. After the "Amen," I eyed the piece of paper in my hand. The writing was cramped and hard to read, but I stayed with it until I deciphered it. "Eric Martin is a fairy."

There was no reason why I should want to laugh. I hardly knew Martin and was not at all sure what the word fairy meant in this context, even when I had, in other instances, parroted it myself. It was just what the boys were saying, and I could pick up that it was certainly derogatory. (I would later shout "Go Skins!" when cheering on the Trojans, my intramural baseball team.) But Martin was the senior whose doom it was to read the lesson in chapel that day. He had been given the dullest stretch of the Acts of the Apostles and resembled a tadpole trying to keep its glasses on while swimming upstream.

It was all I could do to keep from cracking up, watching Martin up there, clutching the note that prompted me to see he was worth ridicule. And then Eric Martin became stuck on the "M" of the word "Mysia" and was stuttering, "M... m... m...," finally spitting out, "sia," only to be confronted with "assayed" and "Bythynia." His hands were shaking more than Smith's ever did when he served soup. And the Bible showed him no mercy, for when Bythynia was conquered, Mysia returned, to be followed by Troas and Macedonia, Samothracia and Neapolis. The stammering young man made it impossible for me to maintain my composure.

"Dear God," I prayed to myself. "Save me. Save Eric Martin. Show us the path through the woods. Pour out the Holy Spirit on our flesh. Suffer not the teeth that bite into my cheek to fail to suppress the bubbling forth of an irresistible laugh."

Eric regained control at last, and this rescued me. I looked at the hymnal, which had never left my hand and opened it to slip the note inside. A year from now, I thought, another kid will find it and start his own laugh. Perhaps in the middle of a sermon.

The lesson over, it was time again to pray. I remembered the pressed flower I had found in another hymnal the day before. It had the same colors as the yellow one I had just picked, only quieter, a whisper instead of a shout. The darkness inside the frail corona held dominion over the surrounding platitudes of the hymn. It floated its stain silently across the page. I remembered how quiet it had been the night before when I was standing on the fire escape, arms outstretched, a book in each hand, only the darkness and the eyes of the flowers as witnesses, the weight of the books enough to still the urge to shiver in the cold. How had I ended up there? I had been longing for home and for some reason had screeched like an owl. Then the dorm had laughed and the prefect, in this case one of the juniors delegated by the faculty to rule in their stead, had been inspired to punish me.

After the service, the students who had ambled into the chapel so casually rushed out. They might have run down the gravel walk but for the sun. Setting before them, it forced the emerging hellions, their headmaster called them rascals, to shield their eyes with their hands and to proceed cautiously. Still in the nave, I resigned myself to the unexpected delay and listened to the postlude. As always, Mr. Flynn was bent piously over the organ producing a mournful sound as reverently as possible. Outside the window an apple tree, its bare branches streaked with gold, looked unready for the season. I supposed in a couple of weeks it would be in bloom and nobody looking at it would be able to imagine it otherwise. But for the time being, it seemed a part of Mr. Flynn's dirge and a long way from the pansy I was twirling in my hand.

I had come back to Greenvale for the day because that was what everyone from boarding school did on the first day back home over Christmas vacation. It was a ritualistic gracing of your old institution with your new self. Former friends, acquaintances, and enemies were eager to hear about the distant world you had traveled to. You were Marco Polo telling tall tales about strange customs, and your audience listened attentively, for almost all of them knew that in a year or two they would be sent away to a place they could only vaguely imagine.

"What is it like?"

"Hard work, but okay…most of the time. They made us new kids wear beanies until Thanksgiving. There are people named prefects, older kids, who give you trouble if you are caught outside without one on. But most of the times the prefects are nice and kind of protect you from some of the kids who give you a hard time…"

"Where do you live?"

"On a hospital bed in a cubicle. It's a little like camp and the radiators bang at night. And some kids cry at first. They read us stories before the lights go out. John Buchan's *Thirty Nine Steps* was my favorite. The food is good and I played football…"

"Do you miss home?"

"No, not really."

That would come soon, when I had to go back in January. On the last night of Christmas vacation I lay on my bed hoping that the sobs I never allowed myself at school would sink into my mother's heart and weigh her down so much that she would keep me home forever. Not that I had ever said anything directly. As far as she knew, I had no complaints and had come back appealingly more mature.

Holding court for my former classmates at recess, though, helped give me a sophisticated air. I had been the first of them to go away, and they looked on me with a little awe. My old friends were suspicious, my old rivals suddenly respectful. All were impressed with the casual way I used my new lexicon: "suave," "hacker," "fairy." They wanted to hear more, too, but the bell rang and they had to head off to class. I was left alone, straggling behind them, turning off at the empty gym. I remembered games of

Simple Simon there. *Simon says, put your hands on yourself. Simon says, do four knee bends. Do jumping jacks.* Even with the eight-foot baskets, I was not much of a scorer, and behind the echo of the gym teacher's voice the ball bounced away from the rim. Frustrated, I concentrated on dribbling.

I thought of the time in third grade, when new to the school, I had announced I could play the accordion. There was to be a meeting that afternoon of the band in the gym. "Aren't you going?" someone asked, calling my bluff. I belonged in the band no more than I belonged on the basketball court. *Think of the time,* I told myself, *you were Abraham Lincoln in the tableau. Think of the perfect math exam you took. Think of how you ran through the fifth grade team scoring three touchdowns and almost a fourth until the boy you had stolen the ball from stole it back.* But the cheers were carried off by the random sounds of an expiring accordion I could not play.

"McIlvain!"

"Yes, sir." Teachers were always "sir."

"Aren't you suppose to be somewhere?"

"Y-y-yes, sir."

"Well then, get there."

Mr. Jamieson snapped out the words as only a teacher or a drill sergeant could, and I sheepishly moved on, eventually winding my way down a corridor toward the classrooms of my former school as if I still belonged in one. A row of gray lockers lined the wall in front of me. They seemed to be inviting me into them, suggesting that the place for me was in the snug space behind the metal door. Mr. Jamieson would never find me there. Not that he would try to seek me out. He had continued on his way, turned a corner and gone off to do whatever had to be done. He had forgotten my presence in the hall just as he had forgotten my fisticuffs on the playground earlier, just as he had failed to notice my absence during the previous three months when I had been a student at another school.

Where should I go? The bathroom, no doubt. "Lavatory" it said on the door. A comfortable spot to be alone and wait for the next bell to ring. There was nothing to do, so finally I walked out to the corridor where Mr. Jamieson was seeking me out. He had realized his mistake and laughed and said I should have told him to get lost. I have always wished I had.

At Brooks there were bells to wake you up and put you to sleep. Bells to move you from one class to another. Bells to announce dinner. Bells to conclude it. Warning bells, fire bells, chapel bells. Someone had donated a carillon to the school so we could have Big Ben's bells to tell time by. You could play the organ into the carillon so that on special occasions we heard our favorite hymns return as bells. John Ross, who was the last of the "seven year men" by virtue of repeating his first form year in the final year they had one (there were to be no more first forms after mine), would hear a million bells before he graduated.

The bells neither tinkled not tolled. They neither soothed nor alarmed. They were part of the fabric in which we were wrapped. We wore them far away from the clustered buildings of the school. We were told that even on vacation we represented the Green, White, and Black. Apparently the bells that caroled across the country from Locust Valley to Lake Forest, from Hobe Sound to Burlingame, sang only to remind us of Brooks, of how to act like gentlemen, how to dress, how to speak when spoken to, how to behave, how to think, and how not to be uncouth, gross, crass.

One million bells. They were the distant jingle that welcomed us as we walked back to the campus from the general store in West Boxford, a mile away. We would go there on Saturdays to indulge in glazed donuts and to enjoy a brief vacation from school life. Normally, we made the trip in pairs, with friends who had broken off from their clique for a respite. Not much would pass between us. Occasional staccato bursts like "Car coming!" or 'Want some?" Otherwise, only our penny loafers scuffling on the gravel produced enough noise to break through the sound of the wind in the branches of the trees lining the country road. Until the bells rang again.

"Five o'clock," one of us would say.

"I thought it would be later," answered a companion, for the trip to West Boxford always seemed an excursion halfway around the world. Knowing we still had time, our walk slowed. If it were May we might start across a greening field, warning each other about the poison ivy at first, then trying to jostle the sudden rival into it. In our rammishness, we issued taunts that led to wrestling matches ended only by another ringing of the bells, announcing it was half past and that we had only thirty minutes to get back and don a coat and tie in time for dinner, rejoin the world of "sir" this and "sir" that.

No one ever discerned the presence of bells on our way from school, but coming back we were greeted by clarion notes long before we could spot any of the familiar buildings. The chiming found its way through the trees and over a hill that the boys who had brought bicycles labored up. The bells honed in us all, producing a hitch in a walk or a wobble in a wheel.

Meals at Brooks were not to be missed, and you'd catch it if you were late. Anyone who had two years on you had to be respected, and if they weren't redressing you in person, their celebrated names were staring down at you from one of the plaques that lined the school's halls. Maxwell and I would have been late for dinner if we had even nodded our heads at the demigods, so we wheeled past them irreverently and crashed into the swinging doors that guarded our dormitory. There was no one around to chastise us, which was good for our ears but bad for our hearts for it meant that we were even later than we thought.

I thrashed about my cubicle for a tie. The space was neat only because most of my clothing was jammed into the bureau drawers. I had hoped I wouldn't have to search them, but the hooks along the wall held only jackets. Three times I had to plunge my hand into the mélange of fabric before I rescued the prize: a red, white, and black regimental with food stains. Not stopping to close the drawer, I raced back out of the dorm. Maxwell traipsed a few steps behind me, and we were both tying our ties on the run. Out of breath and disheveled, we arrived at the dining room and I had not reached my table when the dinner bell rang and everyone fell silent for grace.

"Lord bless this food to our use and thus to thy service. Amen." The scraping of chairs accompanied the charge of that meal's young waiters as they headed toward the kitchen. A boy brought the food out and plunked it down in front of the table's master who complained about the clatter. At the other end his wife was holding court. Sometimes she captured a senior with her smile, but usually she was surrounded by the youngest boys. She asked them the same questions she had asked the night before. She noticed that my tie had not made it completely under my collar, and she straightened it for me while I looked at the floor.

My embarrassment fled when I saw the roast beef. I placed my piece on a slice of white bread and drowned both in gravy. Manners disappeared for this meal. Our heads bowed like pigs over a trough and our trotters shoveled the slop in as quickly as our mouths allowed. Meanwhile the dismayed teacher at the end wanted us to talk about Napoleon or "The Rime of the Ancient Mariner." But an extra helping of mashed potatoes mocked the concept that dinnertime provided an opportunity for civilized discourse. Here I was, a child condemned to skim milk by a pediatrician two years before, at a convocation of gluttons. Roast beef was the kitchen's signature dish, and the meal we returned to from vacations was designed to ward off homesickness. It was the first meal I had ever eaten at Brooks and I remember losing myself in it as a boy named Clough talked about the girls of Montclair, New Jersey.

My first meal ever at school was spaghetti and meatballs, which had greeted me as I walked down the stairs behind my kindergarten teacher into a windowless room somewhere in the depths of St. Bernard's School, already filled with children. Terrified, I'd taken a bite of the food. It was spicier than anything I had ever had before. From my years of training with m'am'selles, I knew I was being counted on to swallow, to take another bite. That if the food did not go down, my mother, though she was far away, would feel the humiliation. It was not her fault that I had never eaten pasta. Our cook was French and had not discovered it. I had forgiven her and swallowed, hoping that the tears that welled up in my eyes would retreat. They did. I had liked the meatballs almost as much as I liked the second helping of roast beef that Mrs. Jackson had graciously given me.

The end of a meal at Brooks brought announcements. Game scores were reeled off and wins cheered. Once, the headmaster proclaimed a holiday and all of us went wild. But that night he only said that there was too much loitering in the hall outside the dining room, which had held up dinner. I thanked God for the loitering, since it had saved Maxwell and me.

For dessert we had pie, and with it the afternoon with Maxwell was forgotten. We were looking forward to the Saturday night movie. *Thirty Nine Steps* was the film version of the book that had been read to us in the fall, and we were all anxious to see it. I had loved listening to it; having a prefect or hall master reading us a story while we huddled in our covers after lights went out had been even better than pie. It had been our escape into another world, far from where we lay, where the English or the French (Jules Verne was a favorite) rounded out the day. Years later, as seniors, some of us would slip out in a taxi to a small bar near the campus during the movie, a lark that almost came to total disaster when an electrical problem ended the film early one time, and the masters who had been attending it made a sudden appearance at the bar. But in first form, it was impossible to imagine a greater reward than the film itself.

But first, before going to chapel, which must come before the movie, we filed into the same hall outside the dining room, where there had been too much loitering, to say good night to the headmaster and his wife. They shook each of our hands and remembered each of our names.

"Goodnight, John."

"Goodnight, Mrs. A."

"Goodnight, John."

"Goodnight, Mr. A."

The pictures of me at that time show a boy of above average height (if I am standing next to classmates) with a freckled face and a tentative smile. There is little evidence that I was fat, none to suggest I was alarmingly so. Mr. Lanni, a football coach with huge hands and a mind we did not look up to, noted on a yearend gym report that though I had been a little buttery at the start, I finished the second form year a well proportioned, almost slim young man. Transformed, no doubt, by the weekly hour or two of "physical education," when we all obtained our most significant exercise by laughing at him. He tried to deal with our levity with some of his own, but that only caused Ross Hatch to tell him he was "funny pathetic, not funny ha-ha," and we dissolved again, having no fear of this gigantic man who clomped around like a puzzled Gulliver in Lilliput.

We were all little snobs and scorned any teacher our radar indicated had not been bred to attend an Ivy League college. We interpreted Mr. Lanni's apparent need to be gentle with us as stemming from a fear that we would rise up and have him sentenced to a lifetime in the school's kitchen clearing the leftovers from platters into the garbage bins. Small wonder that that this man's assurances did little to erase the image I had of myself as a bulbous bon-bon. It would not be until our first dancing class in the fall of my third form year in the gym in that I understood that my second helpings had done me no harm. Then, the girls from North Shore Country Day walked across to choose their partners and the most dazzling of them all, Judy Wendell, chose me.

After dark, there were more games to play. In the cubicle the "rooms" of first formers were one of a dozen alcoves with six-foot fiberboard walls sturdy enough for Ted Allen, our smallest classmate, to scamper along under the high ceiling.

"Hey, Keats!"

"Yeah."

"What's up?"

"Nothing."

"Whad'ya mean, 'Nothing'?"

"Nothing. It's just, you're chicken."

"Chicken? To do what?"

"To go on the raid."

"Quiet, you guys!"

"What's wrong, George? Wanna go sleepy bye?"

"Sshh."

"Sshh yourself."

"ALRIGHT YOU, UP!"

"Uh oh."

"OUT OF BED, YOU! QUICK!"

"Why?"

"NO QUESTIONS!"

"But, sir."

"QUIET! INTO THE HALL."

"What did I do?"

"STAND IN THIS WASTEBASKET!"

"Oh, come on."

"DO IT!"

"Ouch. Easy."

"WELL, LOOK WHO WE HAVE HERE."

"HE NEVER LEARNS."

"MAYBE HE WILL TONIGHT."

"NOT SO FUNNY ANYMORE, IS IT?"

"No, sir."

"HERE'S SOMETHING HE MIGHT ENJOY."

"ANOTHER WASTEBASKET."

"NOW, WHAT CAN WE DO WITH THIS?"

"I don't know, sir."

"HOW ABOUT HOLDING IT LIKE SO?"

"Yes, sir."

"DOES THAT FEEL BETTER, NOW?"

"Whatever you say, sir."

"I SAY IT HURTS."

"Yes, sir."

"ARE THOSE TEARS?"

"Not really, sir."

"I SEE."

"YOU WON'T FORGET THIS NOW?"

"No, sir."

"YOU'RE SURE?"

"Yes, sir."

"OKAY, YOU MAY RETURN."

"Thank you, sir."

"NO NOISE."

"Yes, sir."

"GOODNIGHT."

"Goodnight."

By second form, we were still in cubicles, but they were in the dorm we called Hell's Kitchen.

"Tony."

"Yes."

"Do you want to come over?"

"It's your turn to come to me."

"Okay."

"Don't make any sounds."

"I won't. Where are you?"

"Here."

"It's so dark."

"I know."

"If only you were a girl."

"Sshh. I hear something. Don't breathe."

In third form, we were in a dorm where the cubicles received a ceiling and a door.

"What are you doing up?"

"Nothing. Just having a coke."

"I saw your light on under the door."

"It was only on for a second."

"I know. I was going to the bathroom."

"I can't get to sleep."

"Yeah, me, too. I keep coughing."

"I keep thinking of being a hockey player."

"That's what you want to be?"

"As long as I can remember."

"I can hardly skate."

"Keep it down. These walls are like paper."

"They're better than the cubicles were."

"Can you believe we spent two years in those stalls?"

"Remember the time you walked on top of them?"

"It got me in a lot of trouble."

"Prefects can be such a pain."

"Yeah." (Pause.) "Do you ever want to be anything?"

"I guess I'd like to be a boxer."

"You'd like that?"

"I think so. I think I'd like to be heavyweight champion. You know, walking through the ropes with everyone cheering, knowing that I could beat whoever it was that they put in against me." (Pause.) "I won't, though. Be a boxer, I mean."

"I know what you mean. I've always wanted to win the Stanley Cup and I realized that I'll never make it."

"Why's that?"

"I'm just not going to be good enough."

In fourth form, Gerrit Copeland and I lived in a large room. We discovered during our fortieth reunion, that it had become a bathroom.

"You slept with a pistol under your pillow?"

"For two months."

"In this room?"

"Yes."

"Six feet away from me?"

"Six feet away from you."

"I don't believe it."

"A .38."

"Where is it now?"

"At home."

"Are you sure?"

"It's next to my cannon."

"The one you shot the crow with?"

"The one I tried to shoot the crow with. Remember, I forgot to open the window."

"Why are you telling me this now?"

"I've always slept with a gun. Well, almost always."

"Was it loaded?"

"Some of the time."

"And you had it in your hand when you went to sleep?"

"No, it was just under the pillow."

"It must have been kind of lumpy."

"Not really. It got so I hardly knew it was there."

"Well, I'm glad I didn't know."

"I'm glad I wasn't caught."

Fifth form, I was ready to strike out on an adventure in the woods toward the lake.

"Psst."

"What?"

"Over here."

"Ted? What are you doing?"

"What does it look like?"

"Smoking."

"And drinking."

"What?"

"Whisky. Have some."

"Whew, that's pretty raw."

"Like it?"

"Better than the cokes you used to bring."

"You remember those days."

"Sure…why do you come way out here?"

"It's harder to get caught than in your room."

"I guess so. I was looking for Miller. He was supposed to bring some ice."

"It's a nice night. Have one more."

"Thanks."

"I think we need some girls."

"I'll say."

"I talked to my sister about it."

"Barbara?"

"Mmmmmm. She likes you."

"I like her, too."

"Want a puff?"

"No, I've got my own."

"What do you smoke?"

"Camels."

"Me, too. Anyway, what do you think if I could sneak her and a couple of other Abbot girls out for the night?"

"How would you do it?"

"I'm working on it."

"I'd like it."

"Here, in the moonlight."

"Beside the shores of Lake Cochichewick.... Well, it would be great if it ever happened."

Neither Ted nor I then mentioned a scene from earlier that year during which Ted lay pinioned to the bed, a larger boy anchoring each of his limbs. (I have suppressed my role, imagining I had been only a witness, but I suspect I had a leg.) A few minutes before we had been just hanging out in his room in our small dorm, empty that afternoon. Somehow we ended up talking about size and how amazing it was that he, all of five-foot-five, had the largest penis any of us had ever seen. The topic had come up casually, a non sequitur from someone's unconscious, for we were too self-conscious and repressed to do more than occasionally joke about such a matter. But then, as if the acknowledgment that we were all aware of the phenomenon of his organ had released the genie from a bottle, we had become determined to bring that organ to life, to see for ourselves just how big it was.

There had to have been at least five of us who engaged in what I can only think of now as a kind of aberrant rape, but which we thought of then as curiosity gone out of control. Certainly none of us gained any sexual pleasure from our violence. No one looked into Ted's eyes so no one knew what he watched as he endured his humiliation. A few years before it would have been a pink belly, the right hand of Stan Smith turning its victim's stomach salmon. But this time there was no sound as it did its work.

Ted's struggle, epic at first, his body twisting every which way as he yelled, "You bastards are all going to eat me," eventually subsided. He must have simply wanted it to be over, whatever it was. His sudden stillness suggested he was focused on willing nothing to happen. At first he seemed successful, the gristle lolling about unresponsively, indifferent to the massage. Perhaps the motion was too mechanical. Stan was performing his job with a latex glove and had assumed a medicinal air, and the initial effect was anesthetic. Soon, though, Ted's body betrayed him, the numbness turning sweet; the burgeoning result made some of the perpetrators turn away, embarrassed at the mounting evidence of their triumph, acknowledging their awareness that they were complicit in a crime for which they had no vocabulary.

The boy began to shout, betrayed by his responsive flesh, the swelling that mocked his will. He wanted vengeance. His honor was at stake. There had to be satisfaction. Someone would have to pay for the bone ache. The threats were powerless to stem the growth of what he wanted wished away. It became a monument. The audience, in awe, applauded.

And that was it. Released, the boy lashed out for a minute, and then took his defeat gracefully. At least we had not turned him into a fountain. And we were suitably impressed: "God, it was like a tree." The defeat had become a triumph of sorts, or at least we hoped Ted saw it that way. We wanted a salve for his wounded pride. The reality of what we had done could not be allowed to sink in, to have significance. We needed to believe that Ted, impotent in his struggle, had emerged unscathed, and that we had, too.

In addition to preparing our characters so we could become leaders of the free world (the headmaster had lamented the failure of American prep schools to produce presidents as Eton had produced prime ministers), Brooks cultivated our intellects. This meant we attended classes six days a week and became steeped in curricula that mirrored those of other prep schools. Most of the time what we learned depended on the ability of our teachers to engage our minds.

Mine liked to drift off whenever it was not captured by what I found interesting. I was poor at rote learning and resisted absorbing anything that seemed pointless. There was a great deal of information that fell into that category, though I had a fairly deep reservoir of trivia unrelated to what we were studying. (I consistently won current events contests.) I was easily bored but not without curiosity. Bursts of inattentiveness marred even my best work with careless errors.

In my most enjoyable classes, usually math, history, and English, I showed signs of life. In math we solved problems, sometimes together. I didn't care if the problem seemed absurd—a fly hurtling back and forth between two rushing trains—figuring out something that on the surface seemed impossible to figure out was a good challenge. And when Mr. Eusted described the exploits of Major Mosby, I wanted the daring Mosby to be on the Union side and I needed to find out how the Northern troops could be so misguided.

I understood that history started with endless random information that my teacher narrated so that we could begin to make connections.

Patterns emerged. There was the implication that understanding the past made it possible to make sense of the present. Nowhere was this more evident than in the notebooks that held the notes. When I looked at them I treasured their order and their legibility even more than their utility. They stood apart from all my other notes and notebooks, which were a chaotic mishmash that by mid-semester had scrambled any information I might have needed to retrieve.

Today the type of student I was would be labeled as having some form of attention deficit disorder. Strategies would be developed to counteract my helter-skelter ways. But then I was allowed to fluctuate between success and failure, always having enough of the former to keep me in the advanced classes, and always having enough of the latter to cause consternation.

"Politics is the art of compromise," Mr. Holmes, our eleventh grade government teacher, assured us. This appealed to me because when I took a battery of tests in ninth grade designed to predict what I would be good at, the answer came labor-industrial relations, something I had previously never heard of. I was told that my answers suggested I liked balancing. Perhaps that was the result of a desire to please all of the people at least some of the time. In any case I decided it was a talent I had and, though compromise did not have an especially positive connotation, I approved the concept.

Besides, Holmes was a dynamic teacher with a sense of humor. He enjoyed teaching us about the Constitution, and he took us into Boston to meet the governor and to see the legislature in action. I remember being stunned by how quickly they passed bills, the speaker wielding a gavel, describing each bill, reciting, "allinfavorsayaye, allopposedsaynay, theayeshaveit," before passing onto the next.

I remember Holmes as my ninth grade dorm master as well as my teacher. He possessed the memorable first name of "Dick" and a characteristic that anyone who wanted to teach us anything needed: he never appeared to want to be anywhere else. He enjoyed what he was doing and encouraged us come to life in his classroom. This was easy because as a Democrat he knew he could get an instant rise from his Republican audience simply by suggesting that Truman had been an effective president, that despite his stint in jail Mayor Curley had gotten things done, and that, unlike any Republican he could think of, the mayor had personality. But Holmes did not proselytize us. He had no trouble with us liking Ike though he thought we needed Adlai badly. He delivered his opinions with a wit that made us laugh or groan, and in a way that told us he did not expect to change our minds. We knew he would never penalize us for our beliefs. The heart of the course was to study how government worked, not the people who worked in government. They simply provided the entertaining stories.

Judy Wendall, the girl who chose me, beside Mr. Holmes.

I recall a warm spring afternoon when I studied alone for the final in the room the class was held in. I thought of Holmes, writing part of a constitutional amendment on the board and conducting a conversation with his students. For a moment it occurred to me that in spite of Shaw's dictum—those who can do, those who cannot teach—I could become a teacher.

Though my expulsion ended it preemptively, my final English course was my best one. Mr. Waterston was Oxford and erudite. He asked questions that made me think and assigned books that made me struggle. When I sat down to write a paper on Isaiah Berlin's *The Hedgehog and the Fox* and its critique of *War and Peace*, I felt as if I had wandered onto a strange planet. For the first time my natural intelligence failed me. I knew I would have to work harder if I were to begin to understand what my classmate George Blake, who had always been diligent, understood. I was frustrated that my expanding mind could earn no more than a "D" on the paper, that my paragraphs seemed to fall apart before they reached their ends, and that the pressure that came from being on the precipice of understanding caused me to pay no attention to spelling, punctuation, or sentence structure. My writing mirrored my faulty understanding.

But some things I did understand. How *The Tempest* was a kind of inverse tragedy. How Shakespeare lived in an age where people believed differently than we did in 1950. That to understand him I needed to know about the Great Chain of Being, Ptolemy, and Montaigne. For the first time I felt I was grasping ideas, or at least recognizing them, and not merely recording them in a notebook. I wanted to learn more, even though I was frustrated by years of indolence that meant I was lacking the skills to turn my curiosity into something meaningful.

Although my grades did not reveal it, in class my mind was caught up in whatever I found interesting (not chemistry or French—m'am'selles had taught me to count, not where to place accent marks). Part of this stemmed from my love of reading, sparked by my taking *Of Human Bondage* out of the library in ninth grade. I think I was attracted to its bulk and the grandness of its title and I liked admiring myself for my ambition. I wanted to appear intellectually curious but independent minded; that would explain the gap I was told existed between my ability and my achievement. I had been defeated the summer before by *Lord Jim* so I didn't know how I would respond when I sat down to read Maugham's novel. I couldn't put it down. I devoured it and felt changed by the experience. Not so much by the book itself, but by my enjoyment of it.

I became a reader and identified myself as such. I even recall being fascinated by Herbert Hoover's memoirs. I loved allowing my mind to travel to worlds far from the confines of my own. There I learned of honor and heroism, passion and cruelty, love and forgiveness. It never occurred to me that the worlds that my favorite authors inhabited had anything to do with mine. It seemed to me that Brooks was far from the madding crowd.

Classes punctuated the school experience. In some ways they were a relief. While you were younger, teachers were always more protective of you than were upperclassmen, and the boring ones gave you time to daydream, to find a world of your own. I would draw imaginary islands with airstrips. I imagined myself a submarine captain, a contemporary Nemo. I was a force for good in the world.

The headmaster was not prepossessing. In stature he did not measure up to his wife, an elongated time-weathered woman we had christened "The Lizard." She wore Victorian dresses fringed with lace. Dominating the horizon, she was a kind of cultural Mt. Rushmore who drew those around her into conversation about Bach, Thackeray, and clear skin. Her husband's sallow complexion might never have been graced with adolescent eruptions, but it contributed a share to his own amphibian appearance. "The Lizard" was married to "The Toad." Together they ruled their fiefdom: she with an air of distant dignity, he with total self-assurance.

Mr. Ashburn was the school. After a couple of days of wondering how such an unimpressive looking man could hold dominion over all of us at Brooks, we didn't even question it. It was a postulate based on nothing tangible, simply self-evident. Mr. Wilder had a more resonant voice and a more dignified carriage; Mr. Andrews a sharper wit and a more scholarly mind; and Mr. Kingsbury was both more fearsome and more personable. But Mr. Ashburn, whose beneficent dictatorship had earned him the deceptively affable nickname of Mr. A., was as elevated above them as they above us.

He commanded attention with every puff on his pipe and quieted us by clearing his throat. When he spoke it was in modulated tones. Even when he was angry he did not shout. He simply spoke more deliberately, freezing each word so we absorbed it and shivered. Sometimes a boy had been guilty of a crime too heinous to be handled by prefects, but unworthy of expulsion. Part of his sentence would be to stand in front of his fellow students and listen to a recital of his sins and the acts of penance he would have to perform to expiate them. This ritual, a kind of partial absolution in itself, was always presided over by Mr. A. who fixed the perpetrator with a stare that was more punishing than the paddle he kept in this office. After the stare, he would remind the boy to remain standing and would pause, surveying the room to make sure everyone had joined in chastising the culprit.

Such ceremonies had a cathartic effect. After them, we were charged with a new solemnity and sense of purpose. Our collective righteousness purged the guilt we might have felt from previous misdemeanors. Each of us was accuser, judge, and defendant, and each of us had been saved. Our brief glimpse of perdition had been enough to escape it.

For us then, Mr. A. was omniscient. The reason he didn't spot us sticking the gum under the pew, failing a quiz, or derailing the dullness of Mr. Edmund's Latin class by pretending to be members of a jazz band was that our headmaster didn't choose to. It would have been wrong to withhold such small freedoms from us. It was not his fault if we did not always exercise these liberties as he would have. St. Augustine told us we needed to choose virtue, not to have it thrust upon us. If we were apt to discuss Gus and Sally—two prostitutes from New York who introduced prep school boys to the mysteries of sex—instead of the mysteries of the Trinity-well, we would learn to elevate ourselves in time just as we had learned that button-down collars were preferable to the alternative. His aura would eventually envelop and liberate us from the misdeeds that characterized our actions and haunted our dreams: letters not written home, tests not studied for, tears where there ought to have been silence. His patience would erase the stains of being thirteen. Such was our faith.

His faith, though, was something else. He was too humble to mistake himself for a godhead but noted his school was on a singular mission. And though he knew each boy by name on the first school day in September, he never knew any of us well enough to know how we perceived him. Perhaps he had forgotten his own first days at Groton and his own early feeling toward its legendary headmaster, Dr. Peabody. And this despite having written a book about his avatar, and referring to him in sermons.

Mr. A. didn't show many signs of mortality, but denoting that there were men he held up as his own heroes was one of the first signs of frailty he would reveal to us. Others we concealed on his behalf. It was not his fault that his daughter's legs were so heavy, or that his table always received the best food. So what if he wore plaid vests and yellow-rimmed glasses and that his doctorate was honorary? The proof was in his school. We were the fish eyes, and he was the glue. Why then did he imply that he was not quite as good a man as Peabody, the school not quite as good a school as Groton? Why plant these doubts in our minds?

The question persisted and spawned new questions. One day half the school congregated outside the headmaster's house to protest a popular boy's expulsion. The only weapon Mr. A. chose to wield was chastisement, which was followed by the announcement that the holiday he had planned for us would be withdrawn. Then he himself withdrew, slipping into the far reaches of his study. I pictured him behind his desk, alone. The vast room, where as first formers my classmates and I had congregated Sunday evenings to read our library books, was otherwise deserted. Whoever heard of a God retreating? Gods threw thunderbolts.

Despite signs that he had weaknesses, despite our knowledge of his heroes, none of us was fully prepared for St. Francis of Assisi. For the first time in thirty years, the headmaster left his school during session. He and Mrs. A. toured Europe while we attended classes, played on the playing fields, and found other ways to keep ourselves busy.

As it turned out, the absence of our leader had disconcertingly little effect on the workings of the school. The punishments remained the same—"Write one hundred times, 'I will not pass a note in study hall.'"— as were the bribes— "A weekend away to the boy with the neatest room in did hall during a term." (I won that weekend once, a year after I had earned more demerits than anyone else for the messiest room.) Still, most of us sensed that something was missing. Mr. Kingsbury, holding a bent spoon in his massive but trembling hand and lecturing us about dining room deportment, was comical in a way Mr. A. could never have been. Mr. Wilder's chapel talks had dignity, but lacked the substance we were used

to. Somewhere in our hearts we shared the unspoken belief that the return
of our first family would mean a return to wholeness.

But this soon proved to be an illusion. Something had happened
abroad. Something we were not prepared for. The headmaster himself had
been taken by surprise; ambushed, as it were, by the cross. He told us about
Giotto, about inspiration, about a man who talked to birds. We squirmed
in our pews. It was the first of four sermons on St. Francis d'Assisi. One of
us noticed that the saint's initials were the same as Frank Davis Ashburn's.
We snickered quietly, but felt uncomfortable. An Italian holy man, a Ro-
man Catholic, someone devoted to poverty, had nothing to do with us. He
was completely alien, an intruder desecrating the New England soil, and
it was absurd of our headmaster to present this figure as a man worthy of
emulation. Clearly, Mr. A. had lost his touch.

He did not realize it, or if he did he paid it no heed. The climax of his
talks came one post Trinity Sunday in early May. We sat near to the rear
of the chapel. The anthem had finished and we had sacrificed our quarters,
and while we chorused "Praise God to whom all blessings flow," I felt my
distance from the pulpit paralleled my distance from the man who stepped
toward it. Once he had spoken of morality, now he spoke of miracles, and
miracles were beyond me.

Miracles had always made me nervous, even when Jesus had performed them. I wanted to have faith. I went through the motions of having
faith. I felt the goodness of Jesus. It was in my nature to accept his teach-
ings if only because I knew I was supposed to. If I was not an exemplary
student in other ways, perhaps I could make it up as an acolyte. But I knew
I was ambivalent about the miracles. They seemed too easy and too dis-
connected from any reality I knew. The loaves and the fishes and the water
into wine I could find a place for; they seemed connected to the kind of
magic that had entertained me years before. They weren't serious miracles.
But Lazarus? I didn't think so.

Some details about St. Francis' visions accompanied the miracles.
These seemed safer and relaxed me some. Visions were like dreams, and
I thought of them as proof of the power of imagination. I had been told I
had a good imagination. But soon it became clear that these visions were
different, that they had led to something else, and that they had seeped
into reality. Before he died, St. Francis had received the Stigmata. His
hands had opened and bled, and the witnesses had marveled.

Mr. A.'s voice was filled with a fervency normally reserved to command
our attention when he harangued a transgressor in study hall. Only now he
was celebrating a stranger, telling us of the feeling he had when praying
beneath the ancient murals over the tomb of his newfound exemplar.

"I could see," Mr. A. said, "the bleeding hands of St. Francis."

I couldn't see them.

"I believed."

I didn't.

His voice was no longer coming from within me. His words were no longer the words of my conscience.

"Let us pray," he said.

Instead I looked at the apple blossoms in a tree beyond a window to my left. They were falling rapidly, stripped from the limbs by a brisk wind.

It was later that month that we filed into the assembly room for a special meeting the headmaster had called. He was upset about something, a conspiracy of some kind that threatened the tone of the school. You could see that he was angry, even as he talked with Mr. Holmes, before ascending to the stage. I sensed a return to the familiar. Authority would reestablish itself. I felt like I was taking my first deep breath in a long time.

Rebellion had always been tolerated within limits. Wrongdoing was natural as long as it was followed by punishment. When I was discovered feeding some boys out of the school candy store because of an illegal key someone had made, it was impossible not to tell John Ross—captor, old friend, classmate, possessor of a legal key—everything about it, and in doing so implicate other friends. In turn it was impossible for him not to relay the information on. The system demanded total confession upon exposure. No act was more sinister than silence or denial, both of which broke code. No matter how often I might break the rules, there was no question about my submission to the law, the natural result of conditioning begun years before on the fire escape when I held up a broom in my outstretched arms and knew that if ordered to jump I would jump.

And as the headmaster began to talk I was eager to hear him reassert his dominion. His strength was vital to my own. Without evidence of his rectitude, my submission would be rendered meaningless. He was there to justify my respect, and I was hungry for such justification. It would be vindication for my own behavior.

In his homily, Mr. A. had begun talking about "coming clean." This was the very thing I had done with the candy store—it was as if he were reassuring me about the correctness of my actions. Suddenly he gave an illustration. His brother had been a prefect in a school in the Philippines (who knew?), and there had been a masturbation ring that he and his brother had both been in. His brother had realized the damage it was causing them all and had gone to the head of the school. It had been the correct thing to do. They had all been saved.

The rest of his words rolled off me. I was trying to picture what I had just heard, but my mind was balking. It was not possible to imagine that the man on the stage had ever been my age, or that he had...played with himself? Played with others? Beat off? Choked his chicken? He had been like us? No, worse than us. Part of a group? With his brother? The one who had died young. The one even he had looked up to—that early laurelled head. And somehow he, Frank, though stained, had become the law; though chained, he had become Brooks School. Mr. A., not Master Bates.

No wonder doubts about our institution had surfaced. Its soul was mildewed, in need of airing. He needed to be saved along with the rest of us. We had been misled by his sanctities all these years. Who was there to rescue us? *No one.* At least not here. Not surrounded by the dingy walls that watched over us, the worn mattresses that waited for us at night, the rotting fruit shipped up from Florida each February waiting for spring in the dimmest recesses of a dormitory room. Not ever. Nothing was left but escape.

There is a picture of me that appeared in the school yearbook after my tenth grade year. I am in a reception room that was typically reserved for small groups meeting visiting dignitaries. My career at school was marked by dramatic swings in fortune, and at times I was privileged enough to be invited to the "new room." (I remember watching Don Larsen's perfect game on the room's console television.) In the picture it looks as if I am about to light up a cigarette. I had come a long way from the boy in the woods in Mill Neck who tried to light his first cigarette by puffing out. I look daring, dashing, amazingly like the person I wanted to think I could be. I loved this picture. So did Aaron Shinberg. It inspired him to convince

me that I could get elected to the student council as a "candidate of the people." I was skeptical, but he said that he would be my campaign manager. Aaron Shinberg later became the youngest state representative in Massachusetts, and although I cannot remember the slogans, or my promises, he proved as good as his word and I was elected.

What I did not know then, but possibly intuited,

was that of all the people I knew at Brooks—students, masters, deans, headmaster—Aaron Shinberg proved to have the greatest long term effect on me. The world I grew up in was casually anti-Semitic. Jews were stereotyped as greedy, their features, like John Ross's, caricatured. The only Jewish people I had ever met were my mother's friends, the Schiffs. They lived near us. They had a bowling alley in their house and gave a Halloween party. I did not find out they were Jewish until reading about them years later. The first Jews I knew who said they were Jewish were in my class at Brooks. One, John Ross, was pilloried, but Aaron and Sandy Jacobs came to Brooks when they were older, and they had a sense of themselves that allowed them to be comfortable with who they were. They were funny, they were generous, and they had very thick skins. They had to because the rest of us were either unashamed or unaware of our prejudices.

In ninth grade I told Aaron that something he had done was "really Christian," which I immediately knew was an incredibly stupid thing to say. I was in his dorm room at the time and I remember being frozen by my idiocy. I babbled some more, trying to drown my words in other sounds, but they loomed above me as if engraved in the speech balloon above a cartoon character. Aaron reacted as if he took no offense, as if he heard even stupider things on a daily basis. I like to think the source of my remark was a play, Drinkwater's *Abraham Lincoln*, which we were reading at the time and in which a character says to a former slave, "That was really white of you." But Aaron wanted to move on. Actually, he seemed allergic to stillness in general. He also seemed to find the best in people.

Aaron Shinberg was different from me in countless ways, and I liked the differences. With him I did not ever have to pretend to be a higher version of myself: preppier, richer (an obsession), more clubbable. Like Mr. Holmes, he was even a Democrat. I dismissed his politics out of hand, but I knew that I also dismissed the endless anti-Semitic patter that had been part of my life and would continue to gather around me from time to time. Knowing Aaron made me a democrat even though I was a Republican, a party that I would not desert for another fifteen years.

After Brooks, I viscerally cringed whenever I heard a word like "kike" or "whop" or "nigger." In almost every other way I was still hopelessly enamored of the values the majority of my peers embraced. I loved debutante parties, drinking, name-dropping, and fast cars. But I had learned that bigotry was senseless, not from the institution or the endless hours in chapel or the miracles of St. Francis, but because a friend had noticed that I was not as shallow as my affect suggested. I must have had faith in something inside me that ran counter to the urge to model myself on a 1950's version of the "careless" people Fitzgerald's Tom Buchanan epitomized. No, I could rise above that.

Somehow I had made myself small enough to fit on the floor behind the front seat of Aaron Shinberg's car. I was grateful for how clean it was. My heart knew I was on an adventure. Any earlier escapes from school were inconsequential—my father taking me into Andover for a Saturday lunch, feigning illness to avoid a test at Greenvale—mere respites from the academic swamp. This feat, however, promised to get me into Brenda's arms.

Brenda had been known to all of us for two years, first as Aaron's dream, then as his dream come true, finally as his friend. He had rhapsodized about her eyes, brown; her mouth, full; at the ways she kissed him with sweetness and abandon. Now my friend had given me the opportunity to spend an evening with this legend. "She'll love you," he said. "You're a prince, she's a princess."

Aaron did not need to tell me to keep down, but he did anyway. I laughed and said, "Don't worry," burying myself deeper into the floor of his car.

"I should have put you in the trunk," he said.

"No thanks," I said.

"We're almost out," he said, and I relaxed a little, happy hearing the thumping of my heart. In a minute I would be able to get up and move to the front seat, leaving Brooks and the fear of being caught safely behind.

I was prepared, on this night, to be Sandy Jacobs. Brenda dated only Jewish boys and she knew the names of the three in our class because Aaron had told her them time and time again. "It's too bad she met John Ross," he said. "You could be him, and I could still call you John." But Sandy I would be, in spite of my black hair. The story Aaron and I had practiced was that once as a child I had been covered with sand at the beach and when I emerged my sister called me Sandy. After all, I was from Miami, even though I spoke like I had grown up on the North Shore of Long Island.

"Your family owns a hotel in Vermont. You got the voice in Vermont," Aaron reminded me. "Remember to say mazel tov."

"Because her brother just had his bar mitvah."

"Mitzvah. Now, mazel tov."

"Maxel tov."

"You did that on purpose."

"Mazel tov," I said.

"That's perfect," he said and then laughed. "Sandy," he said, "this will be great if it works."

Even if it didn't work, it promised adventure. Aaron lived in Haverhill, only fifteen minutes from Brooks, and it had been at his house two weeks before that we had formulated our plan. We had been in the kitchen eating scrambled eggs with the wrong forks. When he left, he seemed embarrassed for a minute, as if his mother were too provincial. I didn't know how to tell him how much I liked his mother, her warmth, and her obvious affection for him. Then he'd slapped the table, ready with the plan.

It had sounded great. I had acted in school plays, even though I hated learning the lines. But when Aaron's six-year-old Chevy pulled up in front of his girlfriend Ruth's house, I had more than stage fright. Brenda, who had been grounded for six weeks, was staying at Ruth's, the only friend she was allowed to visit. Ruth's parents had gone out for the night and the girls had agreed to sneak off with us. The plan was to go bowling and then enter into a prolonged farewell.

"Mazel tov," I mumbled.

"Thank you," Brenda said. She had auburn hair, as advertised, and smiled the way Aaron promised she would.

"Well, John," he said.

"John?"

"I mean Sandy. I always get you confused with John Ross. You know John Ross?"

"You introduced us, Aaron. He was nice."

"Well, Sandy's nice, too. Aren't you, Sandy?"

"I hope so. But I don't look at all like John."

The bowling did not progress the relationship much. The game was candlepins, not at all like the bowling I was used to. Half my shots rolled into the gutter. Brenda laughed each time and commented on how big I looked. "You remind me of Little Abner," she said.

And then, as an after-thought to Aaron, "You didn't say he looked like Little Abner."

"And I didn't say I looked like Evil-eye Fleagle," Aaron said.

I sensed that in Brenda's mind Little Abner did not look particularly Jewish. Aaron was as small as I was big, as animated as I was lethargic. He smacked his lips together, gave me a hex, and rolled a strike.

In the back seat on the way to Ruth's afterward, Brenda kept talking about John Ross. She asked me what it was like to be shut up in a school with so many goyim. I said it was bad. Almost all my replies were monosyllabic. From time to time Aaron would try to rescue me, turning to me as he drove, suggesting that I "Tell her the one about..." Suddenly, I found myself cracking the jokes I had heard all year from the real Sandy Jacobs.

"So, I said to my mother, 'George,' and she said, 'Listen stupid,'—she always calls me 'Listen'."

Brenda laughed and I tried to kiss her. She didn't seem eager to comply but did. Out of courtesy or custom, I supposed, for although our lips brushed, there was no passion, more of a bump in the night than a union, the distance between our hearts greater than the proximity of our heads. Twice more and we were at Ruth's, once more, and they were gone.

"Well?" Aaron said.

"Well, what?"

"Did she kiss you?"

"No, she kissed Sandy. It was nice."

"Nice? It had to be better than nice!"

"I don't think she trusted me."

"What do you mean?"

"Remember how she kept saying I didn't look Jewish?"

"Remember when I called you John?"

"Oh my God, that was the end. I though I'd die."

"I felt like such a schlemiel."

It was Saturday night and he was on a short weekend, but I had to sneak back into school. That meant a long night walk in the woods. I prayed that there was enough moonlight to slip through the early spring leaves. I had worn dark clothes for the occasion. After thanking him, I began to walk. I didn't mind my trek; it was warm and the moon had answered my prayers, making it easy for me to make my way. I noticed the wood sounds for the first time that year—peepers? I decided they were singing about freedom.

Instead of thinking about Brenda, I thought about all the things I had tried and failed to get out of: dissecting the sheep's eye, Mr. Barr's French class, Latin conjugations, a report on the formation of clouds. A heap of trials and tribulations. But what did it matter now that I knew that I had found a way to reach the world? If it required my traveling in the trunk of a car and pretending to be someone I was not, so be it. I had no idea who I was anyway. In my excitement over the triumph of my escape, there was no desire to quibble over what I had found on the outside. No, no, it was not the time for introspection or analysis of what exactly lay beyond Brooks.

That would begin on the Tuesday morning after being expelled for leaving the school without permission. I had, along with some fellow seniors, slipped into Lawrence on a Sunday night to see a movie I had never heard of. I did not even have a Brenda equivalent to make my adventure more interesting. When I returned to campus, courtesy of a complicit cab driver, there was a prefect in my room who somewhat apologetically told me that there would be a special council meeting the next day, and that this had been going on too long. I said I understood.

The meeting produced the only action of any significance the council had taken since I had been elected to it as the candidate of the people. We met in the deserted biology classroom where I had once indeed mustered the courage to dissect a sheep's eye and where I had entertained my classmates by throwing verbal barbs at Mr. Lanni. The president was Mike "Keats" Keating, my first Brooks friend. He and his fellow council members questioned each of the four deserters in turn. Three of us, including me, were abject, swearing we would never act so foolishly again, acknowledging that we had made a mistake. The fourth, already on probation, did not care. He was the only one of us who actually wanted not to be here. He had the courage of his convictions.

The verdict was to turn us all in. They had no choice.

"We have no choice."

The headmaster summoned my accomplices and me to his office where, between deep and nearly endless puffs on his pipe, he told us this was one of the hardest decisions he had to make, but that he had no choice but to remove us from the community. We were no longer wanted.

Keats seemed unnerved. He had assumed that only one of us would be expelled. I understood. He had done what he had to do. I laughed. "You know, I forgot I had library duty. If I had remembered, I would have been one of the judges." It was true. And I had liked library duty, enjoyed the quiet of the place and the rows of books waiting patiently to be discovered. Keats said he was sorry the way everything had worked out. I believed him. How different our years at the school had proven to be. He had all the direction I lacked. He was a serious person. A leader not a clown. The perfect product envisioned by the system. When the headmaster announced his decision he praised his senior prefect for the courage he had shown to do what was right.

I was surprised I was not angrier, but then what ire I could summon was directed mainly back upon myself. And even that was muted by a feeling of resignation. How could I have been so stupid unless at some level I had willed myself to be stupid? The school had failed me because I had treated it as a parent. Unlike a parent, it could wash its hands of my small rebellion. Unlike a parent, it could forget me the minute I had walked out its door. Until, forty years later when it would ask for a donation. By that time, among those of my classmates who did graduate, half had forgotten I was not with them on commencement day.

The morning we were to leave it snowed and I joked that God was obviously trying to retard our departure, but a cab with chains made it through the blizzard and took us to the station. My previous trip on the train had been at Thanksgiving. Then I had had a bottle of I.W. Harper to swig on with my fellow seniors, and a conductor had entertained us with a passionate recitation of Gray's "Elegy in a Country Churchyard." This time I couldn't get off in New York and for seven hours had only my dread for company.

At home, I ate alone in the dining room. It was the first time in my life I had been served chicken livers and I imagined they were part of my punishment. All the way down, I had tried to work out an explanation for my exile, but there was nobody around who demanded one, no one to confess to about how stupid I had been, that if I had only remembered I had library duty that night I never would have gone. For a moment, sitting in the dimly lit dining room with a half-eaten plate of food in front of me and a towel to protect the silk chair seat beneath me, I thought that I was caught in a nightmare; that, in fact, I was about to awake and find myself in the library at Brooks where I had fallen asleep reading *Crime and Punishment*. That illusion collapsed as I lifted my fork for another bite and started chewing.

By the end of the week, my parents had put me in Lower Merion, a public school less than a mile from home. It turned out any kind of school was too much for me and one day, when they were in Jamaica, I simply stopped going, feigning a fainting spell in my bedroom at home. The psychiatrist I was being sent to was sufficiently alarmed to say, "Let him stay put and watch TV." I had followed his prescription, staying up each night through the Jack Paar show and beyond.

I ended up graduating a year and a few months later from the school that embraced godsons of Trujillo and others difficult to place. I had chosen to go there instead of a more traditional boarding school because the latter was so reminiscent of Brooks. I knew that if I returned to that kind of a world I would perform no differently. My father was not happy with my decision because it cost him ten thousand instead of two thousand dollars. Still, the money was better spent than it would have been on therapy.

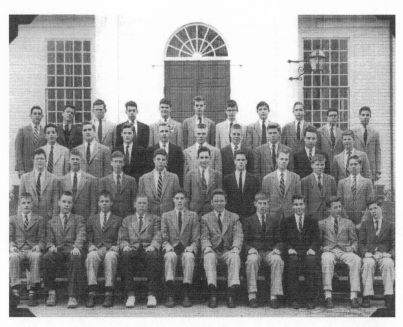

This photo of the Brooks Class of 1958 was sent to me as an alumnus for my 50th reunion. It appears to have been taken when we were in the 9th grade and might have been chosen because many of us who did not go on to graduate continued to support the school. I am the fourth from the right in the top row. Mike Keating, in glasses, is in the middle of the bottom row, probably because he was class president. In general, the placement of the class seems to have been dictated by height. Aaron Shinberg is third from the right in the bottom row.

That George and Peggy were this glamorous escaped me completely.

MATRIMONIAL RITES

Two years before my final visit to the headmaster's office, I found myself staring at a wooden plaque on its closed door. The plaque, embossed with a particularly ornate version of the school shield, hung from a small brass hook. I knew it had to have been a class gift. The whites were too ivory, the blacks too black, the cross too unblemished ever to have emerged from the art room. Certainly, I never could have made it, not if I had spent an entire semester on the project. Not even if I had had help from Mr. Constantineau, wizard of the school shop, who had built his own house in nearby woods not far from where I stood.

I sat down, acknowledging that the "oak" on the door effectively barred me from even knocking. A speech from three years before rattled about in my head. "Old English tradition...Oxford...sacred..." The grandfather's clock opposite me said I was early for my appointment anyway. I studied it, trying to figure out why the moon was rising in the middle of the afternoon. There was nothing to read, not even an old *National Geographic*. I thought about the time I tried to introduce the concept of the "oak" into our Long Island house. "Old English tradition...Oxford...sacred..." My brothers snickered at the words, laughed as they broke through my clumsy sign. Complaining did me no good. My mother didn't think much of my screwing hooks into all of the doors.

Perhaps I could cough. I was only a week or two finished with a case of the whooping cough that had trumpeted my presence wherever I went on campus. My mind returned to the rising moon. How could there be no *National Geographic*? I wanted to be distracted by a young coal-black native with conical breasts and pictures of the desert. I wanted to escape old English traditions and the grandfather's clock, both of which might conspire against me, urging Mr. A. either to deny my plea or not hear it at all. Then I would be stuck in school for another weekend and would miss my mother's wedding. No tragedy, except I did want to go. I loved parties—uncles and aunts talking loudly and laughing a lot. "And, after all, I missed the first two," I had explained to my friends, in my most casual voice. Yes, even the second one when my mother wore a dark green dress she had shown me the night before, explaining why she could not wear the white one in the photograph of her standing with my father on the lawn of my grandmother's house in Manchester, where her veils sweep down past her pearls and past the bouquet of flowers with pale petals, cascading into a great pool of lace that spills out across the ground and beyond the edge of the frame.

As I awaited my fate, the wedding became a dream, a dream filled with fragments. Images dissolved into other images. Chorused voices broke into silences. No narrative here. An album filled with people who were free to ignore history and install themselves beside me in the church, whether they were likely to be there or not.

"Let me tell you something, for your own good. Those colors clash. Haven't you been taught about these things?"

Aunt Isabel, Seebee's sister, was there. She lived in a great house on the hill above St. John's. It was as if she owned St John's. That's where I went to Sunday school and won the softball for being most improved. Years ago that was. We hardly knew her then, except for our visits to Palm Beach. She lived there, too; and we would swim in her pool while she played bridge on the verandah. "Let me tell you something," she'd said, looking up from her cards and over the pale blue rim of her half-glasses, "for your own good." I moved closer, eager for advice. "Those colors clash. Haven't you been taught about these things?"

"I don't think so."

"That's clear," she said. "Red doesn't go with orange. No bid."

I looked down at the offending combination and understood her complaint. My shirt was a red and white-checkered tablecloth; meanwhile, my pants were orange. My pinked skin didn't help much either. My legs had the tincture of the smoked salmon my great aunt was nibbling on.

She led a diamond. "Incongruous," she said. "You need a little blue." I prayed for the sky to envelop me. "Or green," she added, perhaps remembering her emeralds. "But blue is best."

"Taste is so important," came a voice from across the table.

"So is making the right lead," my great aunt snapped. The man apologized and I was free.

Taste was important, though. Aunt Isabel thought her sister's jewelry rather vulgar, especially the Verdura brooch with the amethysts. It was the size of a baseball and Seebee wore it every day. It was purple, not blue. Nowhere near the right blue, the royal blue of Aunt Isabel's blue and white silks, which were gray

Seebee as I remember her: cigarette, jewels, in charge and a cocktail on the way.

and white as we cheered in front of the nine-inch screen, when Bold, one of her horses, won the Preakness. Years later I would learn to admire this demanding, generous woman more than her thoroughbreds. But she was not a champion of children. Having none of her own, she had little use for them. Instead, she favored a pack of schnauzers that had even less use for children and liked to nip at the tender heels of boys and girls between their cacophonous barks.

Anyway, here I was, remembering her and imagining Aunt Isabel hosting a gathering before my mother's third wedding, where I stood stranded in madras Bermuda shorts, or maybe gray trousers that better met my aunt's approval. Images danced around my mind. I moved through them like a pinball. A random succession of lights flashed. Maybe Aunt Isabel wasn't there at all—out of state to avoid taxes, as she was the time she booked a round trip ticket on the Queen Elizabeth, escorted by two gentlemen, serviceable and conscious of their places, one for bridge and one for conversation.

But, no, she would have rallied for her sister. "Oh, Winnie, how could you stay in Florida so long?"

"Nonsense," my grandmother said, in my daydream. Turning, she signaled me to stand beside her. "I've been with Johnny. I told him it

would be best if his mother would settle on this one forever. I'm running out of gifts."

I laughed self-consciously. A Schnauzer barked. "A sandwich, dear?"

"Thank you." The bread, shorn of crust, cushioned some luscious, rare roast beef. I retreated with it into a corner to hide the way I chew.

"Another, sir?" the butler asked.

"No, thank you. I am full."

It was a lie but I was afraid of being seen as greedy. I was learning what it means to be a guest.

In the middle of my reverie the door opened. Mr. A.'s secretary, a woman he would later marry, asked me to come in. The headmaster was behind his desk.

What was my problem?

I had had a terrible quarter and was not supposed to leave campus, and I had to make up for the three weeks I had spent in the infirmary fighting off the last stages of whooping cough: "I need permission…"

I was looking down at my surprisingly polished loafers.

"Of course, you can go…No need for stammering…. Be off…Enjoy… Good to see you are feeling better."

My mother was waiting for me in the living room of our house in Mill Neck. She was sitting when I came in, and I asked her if I could bring her anything. She shook her head, no. I wanted to interrupt the silence but could not find the words. The grandeur of the room inhibited me. The eagle atop the mirror seemed poised to pounce on any gaff. The Sheraton settee looked too fragile for my weight. The tables were all protected by bric-à-brac, precious Meissen animals ready to crash to the floor at the slightest provocation. The room was formal and often closed off, as if reserved for state occasions and for having our portraits taken.

"Do you remember," I said, "our first Christmas here? We listened to Arthur Godfrey singing, 'I don't want her, you can have her, she's too fat for me'?"

My mother picked up the refrain. Her voice was a rich contralto, deeper than mine. She told me of the time that Stokowski told her she must sing beautifully.

"Like Patrice Munsel?" I asked, resurrecting the name of the singer who my brother and I had transformed into the mythical "Patrick Muscles"—a monster that one of us was supposedly in love with.

But my mother didn't laugh. Instead she eyed me sternly, just as she had on the Christmas day I had broken the news about Santa Claus to Eddie. That had been not long before I had been sent off to Brooks, when I wished I had cried out, "I am so young! Don't ship me off. Don't you understand? Won't you forgive me? Keep me here. Keep me. I'll help re-arrange the furniture. I'll…" Now I talked to her instead about Eddie's christening the year before at St. John's when he was ten and straddled the kneeling pad, and how the minister had managed to soak Eddie with the baptismal water.

My mother remembered. But for some reason she seemed near to tears.

"I want to ask you something," she said. I straightened up.

I was never asked, and so her words sounded stranger to me than Lat-in. What had I done wrong now? A rush of secret crimes tied my tongue. Praying time. Supplication. Courage.

"Yes?" I managed, trying to rescue some dignity, hoping my voice would not crack and shrink me back to twelve.

She hesitated. The sky was falling. I awaited sentencing. Maybe I would be banished even for vacations. Asia. I would be exiled to Asia.

But no, it was not that at all. No, nothing like that. She wanted to marry George.

Who?

"George. He came to dinner one night a few months ago." And I re-membered he was special, for we had been summoned from the basement and asked to shake his hand.

"Is it all right?"

I looked about wondering where I was. The walls had bolted away toward the horizon. I needed to find the nearest chair.

"I want to do what's best for you and your brothers. You matter to me more than anything."

My mother's hand was reaching toward mine but was not close enough. "I…" Nothing followed. There was only the sound of my breathing.

Why was I being asked this question? How could I answer it? I had no idea what it meant. Still, I knew what I was supposed to say. The only other time I remembered anything like this happening had been when my mother wanted to know if she should send M'am'selle Zipfeld away. "Yes," I had said, giddy with power. But this time I felt powerless. I had no idea what my opinion was.

"Yes," I said. "Of course," I said, hoping the words would return the walls to me, give me a chair I could sit on.

I found myself asking if this meant we would have to leave this place, desert the fields, the greening grass, our favorite forts, the pool, the tennis court, our basement kingdom, our Eden. "Perhaps," my mother said, and I knew there would be no more Christmases.

The front field vanished, the grass became dust. Everywhere the landscape turned a dunnish desert brown. Mischief, the dog who had known no other home, who I had named and who'd helped us search for the baseballs he hadn't claimed his own, roamed the sand, sniffing for signs of life, baying now and then. I was in the leafless oak above him and would have had him climb to me. Out went my hand, but I began to fall, tumbling earthward, amazed that I was not afraid, thrilled to be an acrobat. I flew toward the house, hoping to catch my brothers by surprise. They were not around. I glided into an open window and mourned the absence of a witness. The tears streamed down my face until I realized that no one would ever notice them.

At a Winthrop desk, one Aunt Isabel had given us, I saw that I was writing a letter with a fountain pen. It would be a nice thing to do, my mother had told me. So I thanked John Braganza, her second husband, for being like a father. I wrote that I would miss him and reminded him of the time he spanked me for lying, thanking him for that, attributing a newfound maturity to it. What else could I applaud him for? His presence? You were great for simply being there? For tolerating someone else's children tearing through your house? For giving your time to help me with the bindings on my skis?

He read the letter out back beside the pool. "Thank you, Johnny," he said. I realized then that it was his voice I treasured most, that I would turn to time and again when someone else possessed it, expecting to see John Braganza in a sports coat, smoking a Lucky Strike, winning a backgammon game. It was calm, elegant; it reminded me of a breeze on a summer night—but not really, because it was grounded, lower, mellifluous, with intonations that had become a part of me over seven years of my life.

He appeared in a dream, laughing at my predicament, gently at first, then so that he had to hold both his sides and ended up rolling toward the pool, then into it.

"Good God," he said, emerging. "What's this?" My father was standing not too far away, his hand outstretched in welcome.

I ran to tell my mother. "Come, come!" I shouted, and I found her in the bath. Around her were a half dozen pint-sized pots and in them simmered molten wax. I stirred the wax for her. "Doesn't it hurt?" I asked, as she painted her legs, preparing to strip them. "Doesn't it?" I cried as Louise, her maid, peeled the caked substance from her skin. My mother's head was immersed in a huge, black hair dryer and she didn't hear me. Louise was also painting her nails. "Run along," said Louise in her lilting French accented voice. "I must prepare your mother for tomorrow. It is so very special an occasion. She does not get married every day."

I slunk away and slipped into my room. It was dark and I had to feel my way to the bed. There was nothing there. I did not trust my hands and swiped with my feet. Still nothing. I had to curl up on the floor. I said my prayer: "Now I lay me down to sleep/ I pray the Lord my soul to keep/ If I should die before I wake/ I pray the Lord my soul to take." Then there was only emptiness. Silence.

Out of the silence came a soft whistling. "Hello!" I shouted. No response. I heard nothing but wind and distant voices. I edged toward these sounds that were coming from a heating grate. I lowered my head and felt the warm, caressing air. I realized that I had been shivering; that I was cold and as naked as when I pranced for M'am'selle Van Snyck. I huddled closer to the grate and realized the shouts were from David and Eddie who were playing with the trains in the basement, talking animatedly while imitating the sound of the whistles. I hollered down the grate, hoping to scare them, but they didn't seem to notice. I sang of Patrick Muscles to no effect. "Supper!" I yelled desperately and finally heard them stop.

The kitchen was abustle. Maurice, the chef, had sculpted a swan from a block of ice and had decorated his bird with hors d'oeuvres. The maids oohed and aahed; his huge cat, Mimosa, meowed.

"Ready, Master John?"

"Ready."

We guided the masterpiece through the pantry and out into the hall. The step down to the enclosed porch might have proven a problem. Worth it, we agreed and ushered in the great prize. Applause. "I bring you… George," I announced, proud of my role. A puff of smoke, a thrashing, then a flash. A gentleman appeared beside me, smiling shyly where the swan held court only seconds earlier. More applause. I bowed slightly at the waist and asked Aunt Isabel to dance.

The band was playing "The Second Time Around." I did what I could to avoid the grand dame's feet. "Your pants," she said, "look a little short."

"Oh, mother," I said, turning to the woman of the hour. "I'm sorry."

"Whatever for?" she asked.

"I couldn't find my suit. I didn't mean to show up in my underwear."

"Of course," she said, "and anyway, I like your tie."

"Bedtime, Johnny," I heard, and then sagged, discovered as I was by my Miss Wilcox.

The last of the m'am'selles stood at the threshold of the room and watched as I said goodnight to the array of aunts and uncles: the beautiful sisters; Teddie with lovely red hair, I must not call her Aunt; Manuel, her Argentine, how I loved his accent; and Gwen, who had seen Hitler at Bayreuth with my mother when they were only seventeen; Aunt Izzie, the youngest and boldest in some ways, speaking up to her mother; her husband, Uncle Dick, who always seemed to be escaping into laughter; and last, Aunt Suzie—my mother's shadow, almost her twin—and Uncle Charlie, always the one to turn to. Goodnight, goodnight.

"Good boy," Miss Wilcox said, approving of the way I looked straight into an uncle's eyes and shook his hand with a firm grip.

Halfway up the stairs I remembered I had forgotten to thank my mother for the party. She'd disappeared. "Fort Briarpatch," I shouted. "She must be there!" I mounted my bike and charged into the night. The rain was blinding me and I slid, head-over-handlebars, onto the ice. "Help! Help!" The ice cracked and no one was there to hear my cry and I sunk into the sea.

Thank God I could breathe under water. A familiar pale blue light told me that this was just our pool. I surfaced like a dolphin. My brothers couldn't stop laughing. "Eeheee, eeheee!" they squeaked and fled as I flew after them.

Suddenly, the ground.

Exhausted, I crawled toward the house, crablike, and climbed the staircase to my room. "Mother, mother," I cried.

She lifted me to the bed. She tucked me in and said that I must rest. "If you don't, you'll miss the wedding." She was in a nurse's uniform.

My throat was very sore. She showed me a small glass bottle in which floated my tonsils. "You were so brave," she said, "now get some sleep."

"I can't. I'm too fat. My freckles hurt."

"You have nice ears," she said. "I'm so happy that they don't stick out."

My throat was too sore to tell her about Kit Smithers. How he had told me on the bus that she was even uglier than I was. Everyone was singing "99 Bottles of Beer on the Wall," and we were down to twenty-three bottles, and he kept saying it until there were no bottles of beer on the wall, and I hated him more than anyone in the world, and I would have killed him if he wasn't older and bigger and if I hadn't lost all the strength in my arms just from the thought of it.

"You have a fever." Dr. Burns had come into the room. He examined me through his dark glasses. "He is remarkably healthy. All of this can be solved if he starts drinking skim milk. Here is the prescription. Two glasses at breakfast and he will make it to the wedding." And then he was gone, and the room was empty.

I sidled out of my bed, thinking someone had been left in the room to spy on me, but no one was there and I had to find my clothes. There was no time to waste. They were scattered about the floor. I gathered them into a pillowcase, sure that I was leaving something behind. "We're off."

My bike was waiting for me. Mischief at my side, we raced down the driveway, past the scattered orchard, past the turn where Aunt Teddie had rolled her car onto its roof, past the dead corn stalks in the lower garden. Eric the gardener, sunburned, smiling, bottle in one hand, spade in the other, waved with the bottle hand. "Good luck!" he shouted, and I wanted to go back and embrace him for all he had meant to me, only he had vanished behind a gigantic pumpkin and I heard him sing a song about the soil. Standing at the edge of the property pulling up the sign with his name on it was John Braganza. "Get on, Johnny, you don't want to be late."

"But, but, but..." I pled even as I pedaled off, Mischief still beside me, barking, trying to slow me down, gnawing at the tires, darting in front of me no matter how fast I went, so that in the end I had to dismount and plead with him, "Go home!" He snarled, transformed into the Nickerson's bulldog. I tossed a rock to see if he would fetch. I did not want him to find Mischief. He brought the rock back to me. He dropped it, panting. I threw it farther this time and suddenly it took flight and he had gone after it toward the sea and I was pedaling again, so furiously that at first the tires spun and the bike remained motionless.

I had to push my bike to the crest of a hill, and then we were plummeting down the other side and my eyes watered from the force of the wind. The church came up so fast I was unprepared and put out both my legs to brake, and suddenly I was flying over the handlebars, not hurtling onto the ice but somersaulting into a canopy. Church bells ringing above me chased me down and I stood composing myself before the church door.

I knocked, wondering if anyone would recognize me, trying to remember the password, then knocked again three times, wondering if the secret was in the rhythm of the knock, wishing I could replicate Morse code for S.O.S. that I had learned in second grade—except I had skipped second grade.

"The girl that I marry will have to be, as soft and as pink as a nursery..." Nothing happened. I pressed my ear to the door. Silence. Not even a note from the organ. Cautiously, a mouse about to enter Mimosa's kitchen, I eased the door open. Frances Stewart stood alone in the center aisle, re-splendent in an ivory gown. "Where have you been?" she asked. "I've been standing here for years."

"I'm sorry," I whispered in my best altar boy voice. "I thought it was just for Sunday school."

"You're forgiven," she said, holding out her hand.

"Thank you," I replied, extending mine, sure that I was right. We were dressed like this for the St. John's pageant. We were to illustrate the sacra-ment of matrimony. "I was held up on the way."

"Do you want to kiss me?" she asked.

"I do."

"You may kiss the bride."

I came close and helped her lift her veil. Something terrible had hap-pened. Her teeth had turned jagged and black. I closed my eyes and re-luctantly leaned to seal our relationship. *God, give me strength.* There was laughter. First hers and then Billy Hutton's, who was standing next to her, and then an entire chorus of Sunday schoolers was laughing. I blushed, but soon joined in, exaggerating so that when Aunt Isabel walked in to learn what the disturbance was she found me rolling in the aisle.

"Come on, my child," she said, as if nothing were more natural. "We're late."

I followed like a spaniel, praying the schnauzers were not in her car. They were not. A chauffeur held the door. Inside there was a cup of tea for me, a Dubonnet for her. She told me my mother could not be married in her church. "Episcopalians think it is a sin," she said.

Her lipstick was the deep red of her drink. "A perfect match!" I an-nounced. She thought I meant my new stepfather, George, and told me that my mother had always had good taste if not good judgment.

The sign outside the fieldstone church said "Dutch Reformed." Inside its walls were white and its windows clear, not at all like St. John's, but not unlike the chapel at Brooks. I was ushered by an uncle to a pew up near the front on the right side. Once there I made it to my knees and clasped my hands devoutly. That done, I settled back. One of my brothers giggled and I glowered at him in silence. He stopped. The organ stopped. The minister appeared. And then my mother appeared, dressed in navy blue, the color of my father's bedroom walls.

"I will," she said clearly, and then again, and then again. Her mother started to cough. "Not now," I prayed. I looked down at my shoes. They were polished and I tried to feel proud about that, but Seebee kept on coughing.

In movie theaters, people moved away, but we could only remain riveted in place by each successive hack. "Go on!" she growled, and the minister recovered.

"Bless," he began, but started to cough himself. Eddie rose and walked up to the font. He cupped his hands together and brought some water to the stricken man. "Thank you, my child."

The congregation whispered. Perhaps it was a miracle, but no. My grandmother resumed her cough. She shook the congregation as if we were the ice in a martini shaker.

"Mother," my mother said. "How can you?"

"Champagne?" I asked the minister. He nodded and changed the chalices. "Take, eat," he said, handing me a mint. "It tastes better than a wafer." I thanked him. I had been confirmed the week before. "The Bishop tripped and almost fell," I whispered, remembering my confusion. "Just as I had expected God to send me a sign." *Bless you, my child.* My mother, next to me, cleared her throat impatiently, and then declined. "This service has gone on long enough," she said. "It's time to celebrate."

The reception was down Old Brookville Road, only a mile or so from the church, on the left, at the Choates' house. Aunt Jane was one of my mother's two best friends. Mr. Choate was a good enough golfer to be invited to the Pebble Beach Pro-Am and was the mayor of Old Brookville. They had a large Georgian house like ours and beautiful gardens that were alive with May colors.

It was a warm spring day, and we were to be seated for lunch at round tables of eight on the patio; meanwhile, a butler offered champagne on a silver tray. I took it in a casual way and sipped, extending my left pinky. There were other trays with canapés and toothpicks, and in the background the laughter of grown ups. Someone was playing a piano.

Seated, I unfolded my napkin carefully. Shrimp were resting on ice. I reached for one, but a glass stood in the way and it toppled. Wine spilled out, bleeding into the tablecloth, advancing on the older woman to my left. She defended her lap successfully and offered me her hand. "I'm George's stepmother," she said, and told me not to apologize anymore. She had me talk about myself, and as I rattled on she surprised me by paying enough attention to ask questions.

There were toasts. Glasses were held up. "In Philadelphia, we only stand when we toast the dead and usually that means George Washington.

But we are not in Philadelphia so I ask you all to rise."

Philadelphia. We would be moving to Philadelphia. It might have as well been another country.

It was getting late. I was due back in school. "Goodbye, goodbye, goodbye.... So nice to meet you, so nice to meet you..."

Into the limousine I leapt. I was perched on the small jumper seat in front of my grandmother and Aunt Suzie and Uncle Charlie. Seebee was not coughing anymore, but I was hiccupping. Everyone seemed to understand. My grandmother made a comment that escaped me but I realized it meant that she knew I had had too much to drink at my mother's wedding, but that she understood and it was all right. I wanted to tell them that I did not really want to go back to school, but instead I talked about how I knocked over the glass and almost ruined Mrs. Cheston's dress, and they were laughing.

Fifty-five years later a record of sorts of the reception has surfaced. There are no photographs of my mother's third wedding, but there is some film footage of the luncheon at the Choates that had been taken by George's sister Francie. She included it on a DVD of her family's outings that she has given my sister Sydney.

I appear to be well dressed in what I am sure was a gray suit—the colors are not brilliant—a very white shirt and a dark tie. I am sitting beside Mrs. Cheston. I appear to be enjoying myself, though not as much as my brother Eddie, who steals the final scene of the film while posing with David. He is irrepressible, slightly disheveled, laughing and then shoving his brother who is trying so hard to be on his best behavior.

Everyone else is more contained. My mother and new father look soberly joyful. My mother is wearing what I take to be a blue dress that is darker than the one I pictured (it appears to be black in the film). She has a small wreath of white flowers in her hair and what look to be pearls except I know she never liked pearls. When she finds herself on camera she smiles engagingly and kisses her new husband.

Her two great friends from Long Island are there, Jane Choate who is opening a champagne bottle and Poppi Thomas who is sitting at lunch and enjoying herself. There are also snippets of her sisters, my aunts Aunts Suzie, Izzie, and Gwen, and my cousin Linda, Gwen's daughter, nine at the time, who is in the pinkest outfit ever made and not at all as I remember her.

I look at the film again and again wonder what else I can glean from it. I have already used it to correct a memory: I had originally placed myself at the reception next to Mrs. Ellis, George's grandmother, not Mrs. Cheston. Otherwise I have found no surprises beyond how young I look. In my memory I pictured myself as I must have been a few years later, taller and more debonair. I know I wanted to be suaver than I actually was, hoping to suppress the immaturity that seemed to break forth from time to time and label me. I was much more the clown, the Eddie in the film, than I ever could admit. The boy sitting beside his new in-law, about to spill the champagne, was not the young sophisticate he played at being.

Emerging from a limo followed by Seebee and a be-furred Aunt Edith
Stoeple on the way to church for my Aunt Teddie's wedding, my first.

CAMP

On the boat, after an overnight train trip, I looked out at uninhabited shores. Every mile, a new, postcard-worthy vista appeared. The boy at my right thought what I was saying was very funny.

"You'll learn to hate every one of those pretty pictures," he said, "but when you come back, riding this boat, you'll feel you accomplished something."

I nodded, not knowing what else to do. It sounded ominous.

I had complained about going to camp in the first place. After all, I had not been to one for seven years and, though they'd become distant, the memories of Birch Rock and Adirondack were unpleasant. Now I was on the edge of glorious sixteen and shipped into the wilderness for two months with no chance to escape. Nobody I knew was undergoing a similar fate. It was the summer after Mother and George's wedding. They were still in Positano on their honeymoon. My friends were all off somewhere sailing and sunning themselves, flirting with the girls I could only write to.

I was alone.

The people my age on the boat had all been to Keewaydin before and seemed to wear that experience like a shield. We had nothing in common. Who cared that I had swum Lake We-Ja-Ma-Call-It at age eight, or that a year later I had made it as an Indian brave? That was kid stuff; this was the real thing. My facetious attempts to present my credentials earned me no respect. The day I had spent climbing Mount Oh-So-Hi, the night I had spent in the woods listening to counselors tell stories of rabid bears held no truck with these guys. This, they assured me, was where I would grow up. Here, no fun and games, no secret societies were needed to keep us in line. Why, I wanted to ask, did you come back? But I had sense enough to decide that they would not treat my question lightly and would instead respond with a communal glower, viewing me as a dilettante for the rest of the summer.

At the dock, a barking German shepherd everyone seemed to recognize called out to greet us. "He protects us from lynx at night," someone said. I was more interested in what protected us from him, but I was not about to let anyone ridicule me so I lifted my duffel in a fair imitation of my fellow campers and walked cautiously down the dock. I could still hear the barking when I reached my tent.

That night I prayed into the blackness, hoping I would wake up at home—

Philadelphia, Long Island, New York, even Brooks. I imagined the past day had been a dream, and I would be able to joke about my vision with my friends. It would make a good tale. I could embellish it, turn the shepherd into a wolf, strip the branches from the trees, and compare the landscape to amputated soldiers left to rot for centuries. Everyone would praise me for having a vivid imagination, but I would swear that every word I said was true.

Two weeks later I was churning in some muskeg (a foot or more of mud floating on some permanently frozen ground) and cursing my father with a heartfelt depth that should have caused him to collapse at his desk in that spacious and comfortable office a thousand miles away. Who else was there to blame? I had not asked to spend my sixteenth summer stumbling through a marsh, attacked by vines and mosquitoes, abused by kids my age who seemed to float over the same ground I became mired in. What had I done, what sins had I committed, to be condemned to this muck?

I almost choked on self-pity. No one could hear me, but my soul shuddered. Why bother to go on? I could claim my knee was hurt, develop a limp that would bring tears to the eyes of even the cruelest m'am'selle. But not to Meb Turner, staff-man, the only authority for miles around, whose x-ray eyes pierced every inch of me and whose response would be to twist my other knee so that my walk would, at the very least, be balanced. Out of terror I lurched forward only to slip on a rock and sigh again. Another barrage of curses erupted, my father still their target. Again I was claimed by the temptation to collapse, and my will weakened to an inert gas. My only wish was the wish for sleep, the wish to dream myself back to my old bed and wile away the morning by eyeing the motes dancing in the sunlight.

A voice woke me. A bowman returning for his second load. Embarrassed I rose again and heaved forward, bringing the canoe along with me. Christ! If it only had wings. Instead, with each movement, it gained a few pounds. The tump strained on my head, and the paddles cut into my shoulders. I wobbled. The voice was clearer and it was joined by others.

In a few moments they would mock me. "You should have brought your butler," one of them would say. The thought of that taunt propelled me forward, shame overcoming frustration for a dozen yards until a branch reached out and snagged the bow of the boat so that it twisted off my head and fell to the earth.

I was too tired to scream, to kick its side, to run away into the woods and find a peaceful glade. Instead I stared at my burden. It looked at home lying on the ground, another fallen tree. What idiots we were lugging lumber through the woods to cross a lake and then lug the lumber through more of those silent, uncaring, unanswering woods. Then, I heard the voices again and yanked the canoe toward me.

I had been taught well enough. To put a canoe on your head, you had to bring it close so that its bottom rested just above your knees. Then you squatted, extending your left hand to the far gunnel and placing your right under the hull. With a twisting heave you launched the craft overhead. The paddles were strapped underneath in such a way that they ended up helping support the boat by resting on your shoulders, with most of the weight on your head and neck courtesy of the tump line, which was attached to the center strut. The canoe—once your light, floating, graceful carrier—became your cargo. It was a hat for those of us who emulated Paul Bunyan, an elephant for me. Sometimes when my footing was not that secure, when my legs were rubbery and my arms elastic, the heave failed and the craft came crashing back to earth. More cursing. More complaints to God about his planet. No doubt about it, whatever childhood dreams I had harbored about being His second son, vanished in the Canadian wilderness. *Eloi. Eloi. Lama sabachthani.*

Staring at the canoe, I knew I could only lift it with a burst of hatred. I would need to concentrate. It had to become all the enemies I had ever had, animate, inanimate, natural, supernatural—God, the Devil, sadistic prefects, Daddy, Kit Smithers, M'am'selle Van Snyck, Meb Turner. For an instant the immovable weight became a feather, then up it sailed, threatening to carry me into the clouds, and I was off again, slipping again, damning everything I could think of, swearing revenge on all that might be hurt by my revenge. My complaints trailed off into the woods and vanished there, settling into nothingness amongst the rotting trees, the mosquitoes, and the mud.

Eventually I reached the shore of an unmapped lake. The others were there, slightly amused by the way I came, staggering toward the water like a wounded gangster desperate to get out my dying words. Some were smoking hand-rolled cigarettes and letting the sun tan their unwashed faces. A boy named Dan was trying to gauge which one of us was generating the most respectable imitation of a beard. I tried to ease into the conversation, but it was time to push on. Everyone had taken his five and had been waiting for me.

Paddling wasn't so bad. I managed to stay within hailing distance most of the time, though my bowman complained about being stuck with someone who had more weight than horsepower. After the first week he had no tolerance for my lack of productivity. No doubt he felt that there was no longer an excuse for my not measuring up. I had gone through my initiation and still I was floundering. It had been funny to watch me dry out my tea bag after our first lunch on the trail. How he and the others had laughed after seeing me, the only rookie, holding onto the stick that held the limp source of my beverage for the week. But that laughter was no consolation for the one who had to carry my second load on a portage because I was still only halfway through my first.

There was no explanation for the weakness of my performance. At over six feet tall and nearly two hundred pounds, I was bigger and looked stronger than most of my companions. That I had been sick for over a month that spring with the whooping cough and that the disease had left me without any stamina did not occur to me until months later. The only thing clear at the time was that my peers were being forced to pull for me as well as for themselves.

Nothing I had ever done prepared me for Keewaydin. The swimming lessons, tennis lessons, golf lessons—they were useless here. Almost all our time was spent on canoe trips. First for one day, then for three, then for two weeks, and finally a month. In between trips we relaxed, ate food from cans, and debated whether we should shave or not. There was a midsummer break when campers competed in everything from tent pitching to cooking. I was assigned to stewing prunes when the boy who was supposed to look over them had a stomach virus. They burnt, not badly, but enough for the judges to notice, costing us that part of the competition. Though our group won the overall competition and I actually contributed my share of points, no sense of triumph could escape from my pan's blackened bottom.

In the end every failing was blamed on the softness engendered by wealth. In need of a role, I had early on chosen to play the part of the indolent rich kid. I was a suckerfish riding on the backs of all those kids at Brooks whose families made mine look like paupers. I had the act down perfectly: the accent, the descriptions of parties in Palm Beach; I was only missing *The Wall Street Journal*. What a performance I put on! I might crumble on a portage, but when I escaped there wasn't one of them who wouldn't trade his place with mine. And in its own way it worked, providing an excuse for my bumbling and cushioning my own sense of worthlessness. I had an identity and, even if it was somewhat false, I could function within that identity. My tales of an extravagant life were more entertaining than boorish, and I was able to make the other campers "ooh" and "aah" and laugh.

By August I was keeping up. The prunes proved to be my summer's nadir. From then on, I began to discover I could do what was being asked of me. I was given a new bowman, Bill Poten, who did not seem to be as burdened by me as his predecessor had been. He encouraged me to push myself, and, though hesitant because I was afraid of failing, I responded. I was no longer inevitably the last. Not everyone noticed, but I did and that sufficed. I toned down my millionaire act and let my new friends take over. One of them thought of himself as "the lover," another "the brute." Dan, the son of a doctor, was already as wise as his father. A boy from the South told us about Bo Diddley and then announced that only Presbyterians could get into Heaven. We protested, but he was stubborn and death seemed far away so we did not care that much. Around the campfire we ate Spam cooked in our own prize-winning style and sang Elvis Presley songs.

This was the month long trip and we all felt a little like pioneers. At one point we went for seventeen days without seeing another person. It was during this stretch that Dan announced that if one of us had appendicitis, he was ready to operate with his Swiss Army knife. At every campsite he wanted us to have boiling water at the ready in case he needed to sanitize the blade. The rest of us thought it made more sense to send up smoke signals and be rescued.

No one mentioned what we might do if anything happened to Charlie. Meb might have been our commander, but Charlie was our guide and our god, half Athabascan and at one with the wilderness. He would scan the shoreline of a lake where every tree looked the same and point out a trail. Even from a dozen feet away, it was impossible for us to make out what lay hidden in the woods. He would leap out of his canoe and hack his way through a thicket. "No one has been here for three, maybe four years," he would say and we would know that once again he had brought us to the right place.

At the end of the day, we would gather wood for the fire and then watch Charlie go to work. He set a log up with his axe and then struck down on it twice so swiftly that when it fell, four pieces took the place of the log that had stood there only a moment before. These he swept to his left, again with his axe, and he'd bring the next log into place, to be quartered and stacked in a few seconds. All of us wanted Charlie to teach us how to split wood. But the summer before, a camper had lost the big toe on his left foot to an axe, and Charlie was not allowed to initiate us into this Northwoods practice.

He did show us how to roll a cigarette with one hand, though. And we watched him as he caught up to a swimming moose and then stood, one foot on the animal's head, one still in the canoe, an animated Colossus of Rhodes. And then there was the incredible time when we came around a bend in the river and saw a bear standing over us and cheered as Charlie casually tossed his axe at the menacing creature so that the blunt end struck the beast in its chest and sent it scurrying back into the forest.

In the winter Charlie worked in a lumber mill. He had a scar on his cheek that we all believed came from a knife. His missing teeth we attributed to another fight, this one against a berserk Bunyan. Of course, we had our hero winning these battles, shrugging off his wounds, spitting out his teeth, and going on to eviscerate his victim. We thought of him as a guileful, swift warrior who never lost his senses; who could lead us through hell as surely as he led us through his native wilderness. Certainly, no one but Charlie could have conned us into shooting our first rapids, a cataract in fact.

Our first reaction upon seeing it was to laugh. But, no, our guide was serious. As a precaution we portaged all our food and bedding, staring wide-eyed at the torrent to our left. "He's crazy," we whispered. To give us confidence, he said he would go first. We could watch him from the bank below the waterfall. "Don't worry," he said. "The worst that can happen is that you'll get a little wet."

We sat on some boulders, shirtless. We had had weeks of perfect weather. The frosts at night had depleted the ranks of the mosquitoes, and they no longer prevented us from enjoying the cloudless days. "This is better than the Jersey Shore," Bill Poten said, looking over to me through his sunglasses.

An instant later we saw Charlie flying. His canoe had shot through the air and he, always a bowman, was standing in it like a figurehead. Behind him, huddled in the stern, paddle in hand, one of us served as ballast. We gasped; the canoe plunged back into the water just between two rocks that seemed to spit the canoe toward us, and we could see the smile on our triumphant guide's face.

"See, it is that simple," he yelled, still standing in the bow.

Holy shit.

Now came our turn. Reluctantly, I climbed back to my canoe. The roar of the rapid made conversation impossible, which was just as well because there was nothing to say.

Courage.

Bill and I pushed off into the swift stream. We had been told to look for the "V," that the deep water was there. "Avoid the rocks," had been another sage remark, but we found ourselves moving too quickly for our paddling skills to influence our direction. We struggled to keep the boat from spinning and sending us backward toward our doom. The least we could do was confront the gorge with dignity. "Left! Left!" Bill kept shouting as if the Grand Canyon was to our right.

We squiggled toward our fate like an alarmed eel. Suddenly we were airborne above the thunder of the hurtling waters. We were going to land slightly sideways and I paddled furiously at the air. My partner did the same. The fear I had felt before the plunge evaporated the second that the boat began to twist out from under me, and I knew we would capsize. In a strange way, the slippery rocks, the cool rushing water, and the strain in my arms as I held onto my inverted canoe were all comforting. These were all much more familiar sensations than the dive that had just landed us there. Besides, we had survived, soaked, but intact, shivering but laughing. We were the pioneers, the first to follow Charlie.

Staggering toward the shore, my partner and I beamed like two pilgrims emerging from the Jordan. And there proved to be no disgrace in our dunking. Everyone else would flip over, too, including Meb the invincible. We greeted him with a cheer that drowned out the noise of the rapids. I forgot having wanted to shout, "Turn back! Turn back!" and the terror of hurtling off the earth, the blankness of finding myself afloat in space with nothing visible but the ribs of my shuddering canoe. What were such memories compared to this vision of our sodden leader? Here he was, an AAU wrestling champion, a prospective minister, with three years of leading Keewaydin trips under his belt, dripping his way toward us.

It was not the first time on the trip that Meb had been wet. A few nights before, Bob Dunmore had decided he and I should sleep in our canoes. Why not? We would lash them together so they wouldn't tip over, and it would save us both the hassle of pitching a tent and the prospect of being feasted on by mosquitoes. At dusk we set off to a chorus of abuse from our fellow campers and anchored a few hundred feet off shore. The insects discovered us, but they were not too voracious and after a half hour spent discussing how heroic we were, we drifted off to sleep.

It wasn't long before we felt the rain. It seemed impossible. I remember talking about the brightness of the stars. There had no clouds when I shut my eyes, and it had not rained in weeks.

"Hey, John," Bob's voice was calling from the adjacent canoe.

"What's that?"

"I think it's raining."

"What should we do?"

"I don't know."

But soon it was clear enough. The first bolt of lightning sent us scrambling to detach our canoes. Soon we were churning toward the shore momentarily revealed to us in a shock of light. By now the drops had welled into a cloudburst. It was impossible to see even with the flashes. Somehow we made landfall near our camp. Once there, we pulled our canoes out of the water and stumbled toward a tarp that we used to cover up the food.

"I cannot see a thing."

"Neither can I."

"What's this?"

"What's what?"

"This."

"That might be it."

"I hate being blind."

We were both cold as well as wet. The water seemed to penetrate our skin and search for bone. Another lightning bolt told us we were where we thought we were.

"Be careful. We don't want to wet the food."

"I know. I'll slip under here. Whoa. This thing is heavy."

Bob punctuated his last words with a grunt. Then I heard a rushing sound followed by a splash, followed by a string of curses that no reverend had any business of thinking much less using. Meb had been sleeping soundly underneath the spout that Bob had made when he'd lifted a flap of the tarp. Suddenly, we were both apologizing, Bob profusely. We skulked toward the woods. Bob felt so chastened that he said he would find a pine tree that let only half of the water through and sleep beneath it. I found a tent and begged to be let in. My new friends took pity and offered me a place at their feet. I thanked them and pulled in my sopping sleeping bag behind me.

"What was going on out there?" someone asked, and I told them about drenching Meb. There would be hell to pay in the morning.

There wasn't. It was decided that we could afford to take a rest day to dry out and catch up on our sleep. The incident appeared to be forgotten, which it was, until my sixteenth birthday. That morning Meb took his revenge. I was still dreaming that I was gliding about my room at home when I found myself being lifted from sleep in a cradle hold. Heading toward the river, I struggled as valiantly as I could, but it was of no use. Down I went to the shouts of the thirteen others on the trip. I was the last of them to be dunked and they all wanted to make sure that the dunking was thorough.

Actually, the water was a relief from the battle I had staged to escape Meb's hold. The more I had squirmed, the tighter his grip had become. I felt like a fetus being squeezed to death by a python. By the time we reached the lake, I was praying only for a painless release.

The last night of camp I lay back in my bunk at Keewaydin's base camp. In the next tent some other campers were talking. One mentioned that my canoe had weighed in at 167 pounds. Another said I was worthless anyway, a spoiled and gutless rich kid. But Bill Poten, my second bowman, stood up for me and soon the conversation turned to another topic. My mind focused on the depiction of someone who had been put to the test and failed to measure up. I knew in the beginning that that had been true. But I had changed and done my job by the end. I had proven, to myself anyway, that I was able to keep up. On the final two-mile portage I had been the third to finish. That's what I would think of the next day on the boat back down Lake Timagami. And I would stare at the tree-lined shore and not mind that some of my companions did not believe I had really been there at all. I had, and one of them had taught me to persist.

Years later, I find myself living in Maine in the winterized summer camp I now call home and where I am writing this. Though Maine has its share of mosquitoes, they cannot pierce screens. Whatever bear and moose might be in the area are smart enough to stay deep in the woods, though I must admit thoughts of them sometimes take me back to Ontario. We have a toilet instead of a log, electricity instead of flashlights, fresh fruit instead of dried apricots. Rolling a cigarette is only a memory (along with smoking in general). When I write, it is these words not those in letters to girls who had no time to answer them. But even when I am next to Betsy in my comfortable bed, the sounds of the night can be everywhere. A loon hoots, a katydid begins to announce the end of summer. The air is cool enough so that when I close my eyes I can be back on the shores of a Canadian lake.

Such trips are brief. A momentary junket before my mind returns to now, to keeping order in the garden, to a carpentry project, to shopping, cooking (not Spam), laundry (did we do laundry?). I do remember, though, many years ago my son Sam asked me to take him camping, and I was at Keewaydin once again. Robinhood Cove turned into Lake Timagami, that aluminum canoe borrowed from a friend became my trusted wood and canvas double-ribber. God was back as an Athabascan.

The trip was launched from our neighbor Al's dock. My other sons, Ed and Josh, replaced the German shepherd, and they cheered as we shoved off. I had not forgotten the sternman's stroke last used twenty years before, and we moved out swiftly and quietly. I thought about telling Sam how I felt that this was the only legitimate way to travel by water. Before us Natty Bumpo and the last of the Mohegans had glided through similar narrows and opened up a continent. But I kept quiet, unsure of my facts, knowing that whatever I might say in that vein would be, at best, boring. It was better to enjoy simply being there than to try to translate whatever I sensed into words. The day was just like so many of the days of my Canadian summer—the sky an unscarred blue, the air warm enough for Sam to be shirtless. Soon we would pass by the last house in Georgetown and be alone in the widening cove, out of sight of all others except a fellow pioneer.

Mary Rhoda, who was sitting for my children that summer, ended the reverie when she honked the horn of our orange VW camper as she drove down the road that paralleled the shore. I prayed she would stay in gear because even after a month she had not mastered the clutch, and I dreaded having to watch the car, my car, stagger yet another time. For a moment I thought we might have left something behind, but she only seemed to want to wave. Sam and I waved back. It seemed a little unfair to have the twentieth century so close at hand, but I understood the car escort, the driver wishing us a peaceful and cheerful farewell, or thought I did until we paddled under the little bridge and saw Mary standing on the shore beside the boat launch. Ed and Josh were holding up our tent, laughing.

I laughed, too, and steered shoreward. This time we headed off somewhat humbled. Sam, nine, kept his faith that we would make it. I did not doubt that we could last the night, but was no longer sure I could carry it off with dignity. Perhaps we would tip over once or twice, perhaps the fire wouldn't light, or the tent not pitch. What if it rained? The cloudless sky disappeared, replaced by a pile of cottony cumulus to the west. The wind picked up. Sam untied the shirt he had wrapped around his waist and put it on. The last house had dropped from view and with it the last dock. The shore looked too rocky to land on, the ground seemed too steep for any campsite. One of the small islands we passed had no clearing; laundry and a red tent already occupied a second. We had to keep on paddling. My arms were growing leaden and I started to remember Keewaydin as it really was, not as I glorified it.

We camped on a peninsula about two miles farther up on the eastern shore. Our landing was awkward; Sam slipped on some rocks as we hauled the canoe above the high water mark. We had to scramble up a bank and he slipped again, this time scudding into me as he lost his grip. I helped him up, but by the time we found a clearing, we'd had to walk through a maze of brambles, and his shorts had offered less protection than my blue jeans. By now he was complaining, trying to nurse his slightly twisted ankle and fend off the hungry mosquitoes simultaneously. I wondered if he wanted to travel back but did not ask. Instead, I offered to get all the stuff from the canoe and save him a trip. His nod told me that was fine with him, and I took off to do for him just what my first bowman was apt to do for me so many summers before. "Get the mosquito stuff!" he yelled. At least, I thought, he isn't cursing his father at each bite or for each scratch.

By the time I had retrieved our goods, all was well. The only question was what to do next. We set up the tent, laying claim to the land in that way. It was an easy job and the finished structure made us feel we had a place to return to, flimsy and lopsided as it may have been. Our adventurous spirit had come back and we went off exploring, finding a dried up streambed that we walked along before reaching a deserted orchard, its trees filled with small green apples. That was as far as we went, afraid perhaps of finding an occupied farmhouse or some other proof that we had not completely escaped civilization. Besides, we had gotten off later that expected, and we did know how long it would take to get our dinner ready. We needed to return to our camp.

Our tent greeted us, welcoming and reassuring. We gathered some wood that was scattered around the side. I went to the shore to bring up some fist-sized and larger rocks so that our fire would be encircled. I had not forgotten the matches so we had our fire going shortly. Out came the frying pan and onto it the roast beef hash. It sizzled and browned nicely. Soon we were eating it and the canned peas greedily, agreeing that the work of the afternoon had left us starving. The meal was the same one that I had had with my father after a long trip, and with my stepfather on his sailboat when we slipped into a rainy Duck Island Rhodes on a dark and stormy night, and I have always thought of it as comfort food. Sam was more appreciative of the marshmallows we had packed, and we placed them on the end of some sticks to brown them over the fire.

I lay back in our tent admiring the pink and then purple sky through the netting. It was a lovely evening, and soon the embers of our fire were the only lights that competed with the stars. But the ground beneath my sleeping bag was lumpy and unyielding, and I wondered how many nights it had taken me to get used to sleeping without a mattress.

Sam was not blind to the scene. Earlier, he had had said how much he liked the water glistening beyond the trees of our little peninsula. Now, I wanted to tell him of Diamond Lake. How, at the end of a long portage, we had come upon it and stared speechless at its astonishing azure blue. It was so much softer a color than what we were used to and seemed to us a jewel of a lake, an immense star sapphire. We all swore we would return one day, even if, as Charlie said, whatever had made the water so light a blue had also scared the fish away. I started to speak but realized my words could not bring us there —some destinations need a portage to reach them. Sam would have to see it for himself. It would be better to tell him about Bob Dunmore and the bear.

"It was the last night of our big trip, and we had gotten Charlie—I told you about him, remember? He was an Indian and sometimes we called him Chief. Anyway, the winter before he'd killed a bear. I'm not sure how, and we all decided it was with a knife, but I guess he shot it. Anyway, we were camped near the place where he was keeping the skin and we all wanted to see it. Only, we got Charlie to agree not to tell this other camper, Bob, who was sharing the tent with Bill Poten and me. Everyone in the group knew about it except for Bob Dunmore.

"The idea was to spend the evening telling strange stories of wild animals and get Bob Dunmore all worked up. He was the kind of guy who'd believe anything you said, super gullible, so it wasn't hard to get him to believe that the woods were teeming with grizzlies even though we all knew there were no grizzlies in that part of Canada. There was a host of, 'What would you do if?' kind of questions. Most of us decided that the best defense was to play possum. Not Dunmore. He'd strike back, he said.

"Poten and I laughed at him. Just then we heard a noise and ignored it; then there was another noise, a brushing sound along the wall of the tent. 'What's that?' I asked, letting my voice rise.

"We didn't need to be very good actors because Dunmore was already so worked up. It was all we could do to keep him from charging out into the night. When the skin came up against the netting, it was too much. Bob grabbed for his knife and started sweating. 'No, you'll get us all eaten!' Poten shouted.

"I started to break up along with those outside the tent. Dunmore still hadn't caught on and he started waving his knife about so that Poten and I got a little frightened and told him it was all a joke. 'Real funny,' Dunmore said, and then asked us how we could be sure it was a joke. 'Maybe the joke's on you,' he mumbled as he sheathed his knife."

Sam didn't seem to enjoy my story as much as I enjoyed telling it. It was dark now and there wasn't much to do except go to sleep. Dawn would come soon enough and we would no doubt be up with it, whether or not I was used to the hard earth by then. It was best to rest up and save my stories for the next day.

"Good night," I said, but he was already asleep. I listened, wondering if I would hear a shuffling sound; a breaking twig sat me up. I touched the Swiss Army knife in my pocket then started to laugh at myself. I relaxed. It was very quiet. We were away from the sounds of traffic. There was a chill in the air reminiscent of Canada. (It turned out to be a record low for July 29.) I told myself I soon would be sleeping as soundly as my son.

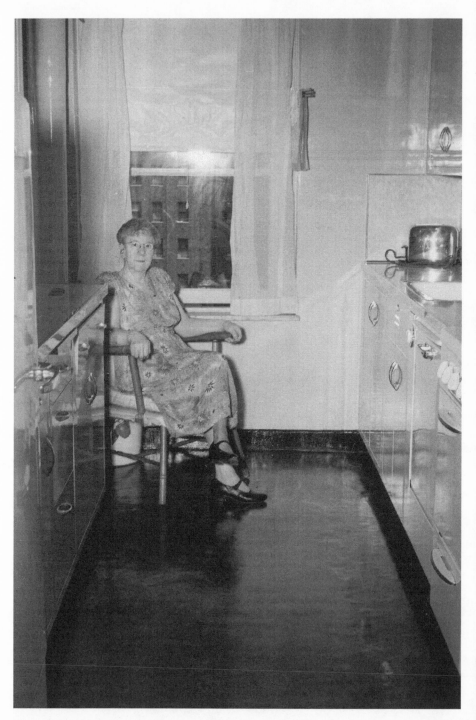

Lizzie at the end of her immaculate kitchen.

GIRLS

I suspect that ninth grade boys in the 1950s were about as sexually knowl-
edgeable as sixth grade boys at the beginning of the second decade of
the twenty-first century. Or at least those ninth grade boys who had spent
three years in an all boys boarding school and picked up most of what they
knew from listening to tenth grade boys and reading dog-eared copies
of Henry Miller (we predated *Playboy*; any nude photography came ex-
clusively from *National Geographic*). Today the Internet overwhelms the
imagination with images; then the imagination wove fantasies based on
lingerie ads: *I dreamed I swayed the jury in my Maidenform bra*. Girls were
other, and their interests, their lives, and their sexual nature were a complete unknown. We spoke of them as objects, and we thought of them as
mysteries. We were incapable of imagining that girls might desire us as we
did them. We talked of them as if our only option was to conquer them.
They needed to say "No!" and we needed to vanquish their refusal with all
the weapons at our command.

I was innocent, gullible, and naïve and had only hazy notions of what
those weapons might be. My actual interactions with girls were not com-
bative and so there was little connection between what I heard at Brooks
and what I had experienced elsewhere. At Brooks I was exposed to girls
only in brief bursts under controlled circumstances—the rumor was they
put saltpeter in the milk.

Lizzie looked at me in my new tuxedo and nodded in approval. She was my
father's maid and cook, and had been my grandmother's before that. English to the core, Lizzie had very clear ideas of what was proper and what
was not. And no matter how I might think or act when away from her, I
deferred to her judgment when in her presence. Her moral force was such
that it quashed any challenge before I could even think of one. The clothes

I left scattered about my mother's house were never found in my father's apartment. Such sloppiness would have been deemed a character defect, and Lizzie saw David, Eddie, and me as her children: perfect, polished, and polite. We would do almost anything not to disappoint her.

I strutted around like a peacock in monochromatic plumage, and she told me how handsome I looked, which puffed me up a little more. She said that when I came in I would find some ginger ale and grape juice on the bar, and some of her cookies on a plate beside them. She always did the same for my father, she added, as if that piece of information conferred manhood upon me.

I thanked her, appreciative of the elevating effect her words had on me; besides, I loved those cookies, brown and crumbly and sweet—evidence along with her Yorkshire pudding that Lizzie was the best cook in the world. And though my father often suggested that she overdid the meat, his children would have none of it. Even the butter that formed the undercoating for all her sandwiches, including peanut butter and bacon, was somehow better than normal butter.

Now she said, "Go show your father." But the door to his room was shut. He, too, was stepping out that night, and I decided to let him dress in peace. Lizzie's frown told me she was disappointed. She must have wanted to witness the expression on his face when he saw me. Now she would have to busy herself back in her pantry. I was tempted to ask her to sit with me in the living room and wait for him, but I knew she would have been shocked by the suggestion. It was not her place, and place was the cornerstone of her ethic. I would have to wait by myself. Yet I did not want to be alone; talking with a half-deaf, eighty-year-old remnant of England's serving class seemed much more desirable.

A year and a half before I had seen Hope Leonard walking down the beach and thought that Venus lived in Newport. Now, she had chosen me to be her escort at a dance, a sure sign of victory over all the other suitors who had knocked on her door. Just that afternoon she had spent two hours in a movie theater wrapped around me like a vine. I ought to have been in a trance just anticipating the sight of her shoulders bared above a strapless gown. But instead of embracing the opportunity to admire her golden curls, I wanted to be comforted by Lizzie's silver ones. There was no chance they would entrap me; there was nothing about them that left me confused and breathless. Lizzie was not about to have me dance in front of her like a trained bear. Hope had the power to do so. What other explanation was there for my being packaged in a monkey suit?

I wondered what Lizzie had been like when she was young, if she had ever known how to use her eyes the way Hope did. I could not imagine she had, or that her lips had ever been full enough to make an adolescent like me see them as gates to heaven. It must have been early on when she knew that no suitor would ever want to win her heart. And it was not that she would never reach five feet, or that she was born wearing her wire-rimmed glasses. It was something else entirely: a quality that would have her shy away in fear of anything she could not explain. A sudden flight of fancy, an unexpected blush, a momentary quickening of her pulse... no, no, no. These would send her to her room, a sanctuary where she could wait for time to find her and restore her to herself.

Or, maybe Lizzie had had a bevy of beaus who had courted her quite properly, standing outside the front door with flowers in their hands. And maybe there was one who had been more special than the rest, one who had smiled at her in church and brought her a box of Cadbury's at Easter, one who won her fairly and then ran off to Africa to fight the Boers, leaving her to weep at the windowsill. Possible. But it was more likely that she just felt that Dartford, the dark and cheerless English mill town where she had lived, offered no future. Not that her reasons for leaving her home mattered any longer. She wore lipstick only on Sundays and not for those she loved. For us she was always in uniform and from the way she played her part, she let us know how much she cared. And we—my father, and David, Eddie, and I—all flattered her in turn and fed her fragile vanities with our admiration of her sherry-creamed chicken hash and the gleaming silver forks.

It would have been much better to forget going out and instead to invite my girlfriend to dinner at home. To sit across the table and make Hope stammer through a meal. But that was not to be. Months before she had asked me to take her to this dance. Her parents sanctioned it. Mine thought it appropriate for me at fifteen to escort Hope at fourteen to a junior cotillion. This was a new extension of our fine romance, a way to elevate the secrets of the Bijou theater and brighten the corners of our passion with lights from chandeliers. I was sure she was excited, ever so much as I was not, for the illumination.

The problem was that everything seemed splendid in the dark. I thought of the cab that took us from the movies to her home one summer night in Newport. She sat so close to me then that it was hard to tell where she left off and I began. The radio was on, a Presley ballad perhaps, though it was the summer before "Love Me Tender." The streetlights revealed her face as we passed beside them and I would glimpse it only half an inch away from mine before the darkness took it away again. Then my eyes shut and we kissed, my mind startled; I didn't know that this was what it was like, but my tongue adept, a quick learner, tunneled into her dark mouth on and on until we reached her house and it was time again to breathe. The pleasure overwhelmed my surprise at her experience (when he told me years later I didn't know whether to damn or thank Brett Robinson).

When I heard my father's door open, I stood, shaken from my reverie, hoping that he would think that I looked well enough to make him proud of his oldest son. When he saw me standing there, not slouching but tall and straight for a change, he raised his eyebrows as if witnessing a minor miracle. I asked if my tie was crooked. "No," he said, and then kidded me about my hair, the polished pompadour that the fusion of my cowlick and Vitalis had produced.

Lizzie watched us leave. She stood at the door as we stepped into the elevator. My father told her not to worry, and she looked at us as if to say, "Worry? How could I worry? Two men such as you could conquer Camelot." The doors shut before there was time to signal, "But I am leaving Camelot. Why can't I stay?" The elevator dropped away, and Lizzie's face remained only as an imprint.

I was a sheep in wolf's clothing as I walked beside Hope into the ballroom. Oh, she was dazzling all right—the sequins on her gown outshone the candelabra's crystals, and her bare shoulders made me wobble at the knees. I felt, as I cupped her elbow, a study in elegance. But suddenly I sensed my hand had transformed into a clumsy paw—that I was no longer the boy who rushed into her arms, who wrote her letters of longing. I was not even who I had been an hour earlier, when performing for Lizzie. No, I was the victim of a whim Hope had exploited, of the decision that she needed to go to this dance and tether me so she would have an escort. I was her spaniel. I wagged my tail as she produced me for a friend so I would lick the hand of some slick rival I preferred to bite.

I felt trapped. I searched the room for sympathetic faces, others who like me had been bewitched, lured to this palace and trained to fawn. As if on call Jimmy Lanier appeared. He laughed to see me all dressed up. Although he looked the same, he clearly had avoided bondage. He seemed to be there only to disrupt the polite smiles and sabotage the curtsies with guffaws. Pan had invaded the cotillion and indicated he would like to serve me. "What are you doing here?" he asked, after Hope had fled to the powder room. She, like me, knew him from Newport and knew he meant trouble. "You are the last one I'd expect in such a dump. We ought to get away as soon as possible and have some fun. The city's at our feet."

His assurance was as patent as my lack of it. He wore it as easily as Lizzie wore her uniform. It dominated his evening clothes much as my evening clothes dominated me. I envied his spirit and he could tell.

"Well," he asked, "what's stopping you?"

Before I stammered an answer, Hope reappeared and Jimmy nodded knowingly and gave a little wave, an elegant gesture, which said, "Poor boy. So much the mouse already. Really, pal, I'm disappointed. Didn't think you were the type. Ta-ta."

Hope wasn't blind and her translation was the same as mine. When Jimmy left she asked me what I saw in him. She said he seemed a clown, a kind of small time Clarabell, except unlike Howdy Doody's mute sidekick, he never stopped talking. Immature. Afraid of girls, of liking them, of being liked in turn. An oversized third grader still scorning anyone in a skirt.

All true enough. I offered no defense. She wondered at my gloomy deference and asked if anything was wrong. "No, no. Nothing is wrong," I said. "It's just a mood." She seemed to accept my explanation. At least she didn't press me any further, perhaps alert to the third grader inside me struggling to escape. For the moment I was grateful not to conjure up excuses for my condition. The last thing I needed was to have to invent a poignant anecdote to make my silence legitimate:

"On a night like this ten years before I left my teddy bear on a train; we never found him." Or, "One of my grandmothers is dead. I cried the day she died but not the day I sat down on a bee." Or, maybe best... "The day I cried the most I thought I had died from showing off. I had jumped down from an old car's running board and slid beneath its wheels. It stopped, a miracle, but for an hour I wasn't sure it had and wailed, imagining I had seen the wheels crush my legs into the gravel on Cobb Avenue between Mrs. Snowden's morning glories and the back gate to my grandmother's house in Manchester." Or, maybe I could share something from the other sad times, when tears hadn't come, but when I'd felt alone. "Deedee Martin from the class above never looked at me. She had a goddess's flaxen hair and suffered when I waltzed with her at dancing class."

Okay, not that one—Hope would get jealous. But this got me thinking about the time just before I was sent away to boarding school, when I was consigned to dancing class, wanting to be bad enough to join those Mr. Durham had exiled to an outer room for being insufficiently polite.

We had always assembled on Friday afternoons. Earlier we would have been dropped off at home to be scrubbed and hustled into the clothes reserved only for Sunday school and dancing class. M'am'selle would chauffeur us to Piping Rock, picking up some fellow victims along the way. We were uncharacteristically mute, subdued by the combination of terror at the thought of girls and greater terror at the severity of Mr. Durham, the martinet responsible for transforming us from almost normal fifth graders into little gentlemen.

Deportment was everything. In the car, clean and suited, laced in shiny black leather shoes, we sat upright and stared straight ahead as if practicing for the ballroom chairs that awaited us. Mr. Durham liked to complain that we did not know how to sit, a hand on each knee, alternating with the girls, who had to sit with ankles crossed, just so, the way Miss Chapin, later to become Mrs. Durham, sat.

The chairs extended in lines that ran along two walls in the large reception room, which was completed with damask curtains and chandeliers and usually reserved for dinners and parties we were too young to attend. Between Mr. Durham and us lay a dance floor we would occupy from time to time, gazing over or into the shoulder of our partner whose gloved right hand rested on her partner's left shoulder. We were instructed to move our feet precisely in steps that were appropriate for the specific dance—foxtrot or waltz; rumba or tango. We stood as far apart as it was possible to stand while still maintaining contact.

We would practice each step—one-two-three, one-two-three-four—until someone's incompetence would frustrate Mr. Durham. Sometimes this was the result of inattention, but often it was rooted in rebellion: a deliberate attempt to step on a girl's foot, a stumble, a snicker, a laugh, a suddenly sprained ankle, a desperate plea for escape. Disruption usually meant being sent from the room to a holding area presided over by a dutiful mother who, with any luck, was not a particularly impressive disciplinarian.

Only boys were exiled. The girls by nature seemed to have a better sense of why we were there in the first place. We knew most of them from school, all except a handful who went to Eastwoods and were seen as mysterious and beautiful. We believed that these girls were who they appeared to be. Our classmates from Greenvale, on the other hand, had acquired a new identity. We had previously known them as not-boys. Now they seemed transformed by the alien world of dancing class, and we sensed they were suddenly embarrassed by our hopeless awkwardness. The roles of the sexes were reversed. We were not-girls. This was our initiation into a world our parents indicated we were meant to embrace. The experience was disorienting, and though we were far from being able to express our feelings, we sensed the unfairness of it all.

The reward for those who endured the hour was a demonstration of the dance of the day by Mr. Durham and Miss Chapin. The distance between the dance they tried to teach us to do and the dance they performed was infinite. The woodenness of what we had learned disappeared in their first steps. They whirled dancing tightly together, swiftly, keeping pace with the piano, dazzlingly close, filling the entire floor with a kind of freedom and joy no matter how intricate the footwork. I remember being taken away by their dancing. As soon as the music stopped, the spell lifted, and I needed to squirm in my chair, catch someone else's eye, stick my tongue out, groan, laugh, escape.

Dancing class faded from memory, and I chose not to share that excuse for my mood either, even as I noted that Hope sat on my left frowning at me. I took a bite of the cream chicken. It was pasty, and I longed for Lizzie's. I added that to my burgeoning list of grievances. I wanted to lay each pathetic happening in my life at my girl's feet, but I could see that Hope had lost all patience with my sour countenance—there was no proper explanation for it. She gave me her back and began listening to George Moore, a friend a year ahead of me at Brooks who was seated on her left. He had found a way to get some pleasure from the evening.

After the creamed chicken was whisked away, Hope went off to dance with him. It was the second time she had done so, the second time I had failed to ask her first. I sat fast, trying to be jealous. She laughed too quickly at his jokes. And now she pressed against him just too much. That seemed sufficient cause to latch onto Lanier, to fly away, to rush into the night and not look back, to flee. And so I did. I left the dance, and Hope, behind me.

"John." There was an edge to my father's voice that cut through me.

"Yes," I mumbled, barely audibly.

"Please come in here."

I recognized the tone. It was the same one I had first heard years before when I'd refused to see *Annie Get Your Gun* a second time. I remembered how I had been afraid of all the shooting.

I slunk toward my father's room. He was sitting on his bed. He had untied his tie and it hung around his neck and dangled down his shirt.

"Where have you been?" he asked. I had no answer and stood there, head bowed. Not until now, as I write this, have I thought he might have been as alarmed as I was once when one of my sons stayed out late enough to panic me.

"It's after twelve," he said.

"I went to the movies," I confessed, wishing that instead of pursuing the conversation we would have, I could tell him about *The Prisoner*, that it was a good movie and Alec Guinness played a cardinal in it, one who went to prison and was driven to admit to crimes he never had committed.

"Mrs. Leonard called me."

I forgot about the film and looked at the rug's design beneath my feet. "Oh," I heard myself say.

"She said Hope was very upset that you left her at the dance."

Hope's face appeared and disappeared. I wondered what to say next. What if I lied and said the doorman wouldn't let me in again; that I had just stepped out to catch a little air?

"She thought that I should know."

"I understand."

"I don't," my father said, the anger resurfacing in his voice. I remembered how, on the afternoon I was supposed to be at *Annie Get Your Gun* I had played cards with his mother. It was about a year before she died, and she seemed frail and gray, but I was Old Maid more frequently than she was. When we had finished, Lizzie had brought out some cookies and we had eaten them quietly, enjoying each and every bite.

"How could you be so..." he paused, searching for a word, "inconsiderate?" And then he added, "Rude?"

The questions sounded genuine. My action had been beyond his ken. Mine, too, I thought. I didn't understand myself.

"Hope got home okay?" I asked. Her face came back to me. It was tearful, and filled with scorn.

"Eventually," my father sighed. "She had to phone her mother."

"I'm sorry," I said, studying the carpet once again.

"Well, that's the least you should be. I want you to write letters of apology to both Hope and Mrs. Leonard."

"Now?" I asked.

"No, in the morning," he replied.

"I will," I said, as if to show him that I had a choice and had chosen wisely.

"Good night," he said.

"That's all?"

"That's all for now," he said, and then, just as I was closing the door, he added, "You better have some of those cookies. I don't want to have Lizzie all upset in the morning."

I did. They eased the pain a little. They made me six again. Lizzie would ask me how I was after breakfast. I would have to find something good to say.

I wondered if Hope had cried. Just that afternoon we had been so close, and suddenly we would never touch again. "Forgive me," I whispered in the dark, but only the whining of the wintery wind answered me. At least, I thought, I had hung my suit up nicely.

I eased toward sleep trying to think of some things I had done right in my life. Mrs. Jackson had said I was polite. I'd lost some weight and starred in a football game. My friends thought I was funny; at least they laughed when I wanted them to laugh. One teacher had said I had matured a lot. Then there was that weekend off from school I received for a having a neat room.

Those were my most recent blossomings. My mind reached toward the past for more. It found the book I had won from Time for being the best geographer in my class, the 100 that I had received on the sixth grade math exam. An aunt telling me once again that I had been brave when they took my tonsils out. And hadn't I starred as Lincoln in the fourth grade tableau?

I gathered all the precious proof of my goodness and tried to weave a garland from the deeds. I repeated the deeds in hopes that the repetition would give substance to the whole, crown me with righteousness. But when I had done with my incantations and paused to look at what I had wrought, I only saw a wreath of thorns—all my faded glories had been shed. They lay beneath my feet, withered roses cluttering the carpet. In some ways they are still there, still haunting me for making such a bad and cruel choice that night.

When Mimi Spaeth, ice princess of Southampton, took a seat beside me, the horizon we viewed was the Badlands of North Dakota. Perhaps she needed me to save her from the ghost of Sitting Bull. What else would bring her to my side? Not long before I had teased her with aplomb and without mercy, pretending that I was a budding Leonardo and nothing less would do than to paint her nude beneath a waterfall.

Though I had no artistic talent whatsoever, such brass required an audience, and a dozen or so compañeros accompanied Mimi and me on our way to a dude ranch hidden in a corner of Wyoming. Our chaperones had long retired to their berths, and we were in command of one of the Northern Pacific's finest observation cars. To entertain us, Nature was providing a *son et lumière* beyond anything man had ever concocted for Versailles or Independence Hall. A spectacular acrobatic display of heat lightning was revealing the Black Hills as monumental amethysts. We oohed and aahed at each flash as if God had exposed himself. It seemed that after a childhood of rumors, we were finally heading toward the Promised Land.

Perhaps it was that Mimi found my arms comforting amidst these bizarre visions, and this despite her own initial scorn, her protestations against my arrogance. She had come to this trip armed with a friend who, most of the time, sat beside her like a splenetic virago commanding my nymph to pay me no attention. No matter, for the fire had gone from Mimi's eyes to her heart. No one was more astonished at my triumph than I was.

Alas, the morning cast a different light on things. My new love's glowering shrew had marshaled her troops and marched them between us, and nothing I could say or do could even half convince my black-haired beauty that I had not made her act the fool. She hissed, frowned, and froze me with her cold, cold stare. It had all been some terrible mistake. She would erase the night before, and restore her damaged reputation.

And so I guess she did. For at least another day, I tried to resurrect her tenderness to no avail. Her grimace had become a perpetual veil. She had changed from my Echo into a sister of chastity. I bowed respectfully and went my way.

That's when the altitude took over. If my brief romance had evaporated into thin air, compensation was soon to materialize. The summer before I had been trekking through Canada; this one I would spend floating in the Rockies. Valley Ranch, Valley, Wyoming, was 8,000 feet above sea level. It was owned by a vice president of Brooks Brothers and was inhabited by tenderfeet and tumbling tumbleweed. There was nothing not to like about our home on the range, a land filled with elk and an occasional tree, a country where seldom was heard a discouraging word.

The only problem was a mathematical one: more boys than girls. But that situation, we felt confident, was only temporary. The Walker twins were due in from Portland, Oregon. Nothing less than terminal acne could protect them. They would join Kitty, Julie, and the lesser lights whose names escape me now, a chorus line of dancing girls there to catch one of the leading men if he should chance to fall. Especially if it were Billy McKnight whose quick smile always made them swoon; oh, how we begged him to be happy with his lot and keep his distance from the eagerly awaited queens of the Northwest.

Fat chance, the greedy rat. It wasn't enough for McKnight to be satisfied with a single victim. He had to flit around like an intoxicated hummingbird, sipping first on one rose, then the next. It made no difference to him that his every glance caused a heart to skip a beat. He claimed none of his victims were really putting out. One had been spoken for by someone whom he knew given provocation might beat him to a pulp. Another had too fine an upbringing to lose her reputation at fifteen. No, no, it had to be these flowers from the West. He laughed smugly like a cocky gambler on a riverboat as we all wagered on who would end up where with each of them.

When it came time to play our hands, McKnight took Beth. Her twin Mary did not interest us as much, as her teeth were kind of small, and she didn't laugh at our raucous remarks quite so provocatively as her sister did. Still, both seemed flattered at being welcomed by our raunchy posturing. They accepted the roles we had given them easily enough for their rivals from the East to turn catty. Not that it made much difference to me, for all the time I knew I had an ace in the hole.

The twins and I were headed on a two-week pack trip and no rival would be along. The other boys accompanying me on the trip were anemic, or handicapped by lisps, pimples, or strange names (like Enos). And the girls.... Well, there were Mimi and her friend, who were busy making sure the walls of their teepee would not collapse and did not warrant my approach. And there was Ruth, who was pretty enough but was apt to say strange things that made us think her mind was plugged into another world. Besides her outraged father, who had come to the ranch with her, had terrified me one morning after we had thrown her into a pond. He had sought us out and yelled, "Don't you see that Ruth is not a child anymore?" His rage left us speechless. As his daughter emerged from her baptism, we had seen so indeed, but it never occurred to us that she might feel humiliated. We, like Ruth, were just this side of childhood. We were carried away by the romance we invested in the West. "What are you talking about?" we wanted to shout back, but though we didn't understand, we knew. Whatever Ruth herself might have felt, she would be safe from me.

No, I had others on my mind. Ruth, like Mimi and her friend, was not of Wyoming. They were part of the world we had escaped. A world of parents, of seriousness, of propriety that belonged to the preachers and puritans on the eastern side of the Continental Divide. No, Wyoming was for explorers—the unmapped territory. Clearly, when I rode out on our pack trip into the mountains in the morning, I would be the chief of an expedition; the twins would be my squaws.

"Clearly," I said aloud, sipping on my 3.2 beer. Oh, if I had cursed my father the summer before for having me up to my knees in muskeg, I praised him now for signing me up on this expedition so that McKnight, Michel, and Meehan were left behind me. I liked my Long Island cowboy friends a lot, for we were high on each other and being part of a gang allowed for bursts of joy rooted in collective irresponsibility, but certain missions were better set out on alone. When I returned from my fortnight on the trails I could regale them all with the tidbits of my journey.

Kitty laughed as I went on about it all. She was going to be headed back East by the time I came back from my trip and had asked me over to her cabin to say goodbye, late, after everyone else had turned in for the night. I had no trouble honoring her request. She was the only girl any one of us could have fallen for (Julie's beauty was incapacitating), and the only one who could have been a friend as well as a lover. She knew how to laugh at herself and had no trouble forgiving McKnight and me for hiding beneath the beds in her room one night while she undressed. "Oh!" she had cried when we popped out unable to keep from laughing. "I usually take my bra off after my nightgown is on." Yes, she was angry, but not enough to banish us for long. Besides, McKnight's view had been blocked and that meant only I had the chance to glimpse her treasures. I recounted how I had struggled to hold back a cough from the second she had come in, but failed to confess that in the end some force had shut my eyes and I had honored her privacy.

We talked about McKnight. How she had wanted him instead of Mike Michel to bring her back from all the square dances. I laughed, for it was I, not either one of them, who she was close to now, to whom she was giving farewell favors. I pleaded with her to open her mouth a little when she kissed me, but she abstained. Bill Poten, my bowman from Keewaydin, had been sweet on her the summer before. I wondered if he was pining still, even as his old buddy took all the liberties that she permitted.

The pack trip got underway shortly after breakfast. There were snapshots and cheers as I mounted Jake, a huge sluggard of a strawberry roan. Jake was so lethargic that he had fallen off the road one day and almost killed us both. Mike Meehan made lewd noises as I tried to maneuver toward the Walkers. Kitty waved and I wanted to give up whatever education the twins had in store for me, but someone made a clicking sound and my horse responded by ambling off after the beast in front of him. I looked back forlornly at the crowd of admirers. The other riders were beginning to scatter but none were following me. "Oh, well," I thought, taking in my fellow travelers. "Despite my insecurity atop this stupid horse, despite the thought of sleeping on the ground once more, despite the absence of beer and my drinking buddies, there have been worse fates than this. Giddum up, Scout; Heigh ho, Silver, away!"

Beth or Mary, Mary or Beth. The problem was I had to make a choice and had no idea how to go about it. For twins, they looked and acted quite differently. Beth seemed the conventionally pretty one, and I was nothing if not conventional in my tastes. On the other hand, her heart belonged to our local Romeo. Mary seemed more interested in me, and when I went with her to fill up our canteens in the Shoshone, she made that interest obvious. She had no problem kissing me the way Kitty wouldn't. "This settles it," I thought, but for them it hadn't been settled at all.

God knows how it started. I heard echoes of my brothers' epic struggles, only instead of boys in a basement, the noises came from a pair of sisters who went at it in a tent—a hissing, squealing, screeching duet filled with curses, gasps, and cries. No song had ever riveted an audience more than this one riveted me. I watched them through the tent flap, enthralled. Instead of punching, they were scratching. They tried to pull each other's hair; they tumbled wildly about the tiny space tearing at each other's clothes; they kicked and bit at anything they couldn't grab. I sat there, prisoner of their war, unsure of whom to root for, captivated by their caterwauling violence.

In the end, Beth lost and lay whimpering on the canvas floor of the tent. This inspired me to offer consolation. Oh, I would like to think that I acted out of sympathy for the sufferer, but I knew then as clearly as I know now that such was not the case. This was my chance to worm my way into the clutches of the twin whom consensus deemed more desirable. What had passed between Mary and me was hardly enough to make me feel that I was betraying her. Besides, Peter, a nice, amiable type, was at that very moment pledging his support to her. What could have been more perfect? Beth was to be mine, only not completely.

Although grateful for my soothing hand, Beth was not overly stimulated by my lasciviousness. Oh, she permitted my groping affection, but never encouraged it. Night after night, I lay beside her in the tent (our chaperones having had long retired to theirs) doing what I could to change her passivity to passion. But she melted slowly, too slowly, and by the end of the trip our evening sessions had just begun introducing me to the unknown.

Meehan and McKnight rode out to greet me. They laughed when I told them that Jake, just that morning, had walked into a tree, the only tree I had seen for three miles. Of course, this was not the story they had come to hear. And neither were they interested in my description of crossing the Continental Divide or seeing the Grand Tetons from thirty miles away— glimmering in the afternoon sun, set above the surrounding mountains like a tiara of yellow diamonds. They didn't much want to hear about how good the food was or how few fish we caught. And they didn't spend any time praising the stubble that I sported from my two weeks in the wild.

"Later," I finally put them off, not sure whether to expand the extent of my amatory adventures or to let them hear the truth, a modest accomplishment, but an accomplishment nonetheless. Whatever I claimed was washed away in the beer we drank that night, a welcome home celebration for us weary pioneers. After all, every other day we had ridden thirty miles or so. We had survived intact and that was sufficient cause for a party.

It wasn't long before Beth found her way back into the arms of her former lover. I groused, calling her a name or two before Mary convinced me not to bother. "Let's get out of here," she said. I was not about to argue. We were all down by the river in honor of the warm night and the moonlight. I slipped on a rock and would have fallen if Mary hadn't caught me. I thanked her, and we walked toward the ranch.

Back in her cabin we talked quietly. I tried to explain why I had let her go, how I thought that she had liked Peter better. She grimaced at that. She said each night of the trip had been torture. He bored her, bored her, while listening to Beth and me moaning beside her. If I had gone with her after her fight with her sister, she lamented, it was possible that she would have given me everything a woman could give a man.

"Everything?" I asked.

"Everything."

It was too late for that now. Someone walked in just as we were about to discover all the joys we had missed.

I had drunk enough 3.2 beer that night to have the universe spin around me like a top as I eased into bed. I tried to slow it down by sitting up. That's when the summer's girlfriends reappeared, dancing about me as if I were a Maypole. Mimi and Kitty, Beth and Mary, all dressed like cowgirls, bandanas streaming from their necks, yodeling, and wrapping me inside a tightening circle.

After Peggy and George were married, I spent slivers of each summer in Maine, not the relatively rustic part I live in now, but in Northeast Harbor where we stayed in different cottages and played at different sports with the sons and daughters of our parents' set. Here, the girls were like a flock of fluttering birds—alighting at the pool, the tennis club, the yacht club— awkward for a moment on the ground, then off and soaring again. They seemed always to be passing before us, clad in pinks and violets, taking us in with their eyes as we tried to take them in with ours. They would tease us with their smiles, keeping us at bay but ensuring we weren't about to ignore them. Once in a while, one would break off and a boy would give chase, only to see her duck into a lane where her friends we waiting...

"She likes you."

"No, I think she likes you."

"Are you sure?"

"I think so."

"What about Sinkler?"

"She told Suzie she doesn't like him anymore."

"That's not the way it looked tonight."

"She feels trapped."

"Well, how does that help me?"

"He's going away in two days."

"It didn't make much difference the last time he left."

"You're blind."

"What do you mean?"

"Can't you tell by the way she dances with you?"

"She dances with everyone that way."

"No, she doesn't."

"I guess you're right."

"See?"

"It's kind of nice the way she dances."

"She looks like she melted onto you."

"You know?"

"What?"

"I kind of like her."

"I thought so."

"Do you think she's pretty?"

"Kind of. But she's the personality type."

"I guess so. There sure are a lot of nice girls up here."

"If only they weren't together all the time."

"I know."

All of them were in love with the summer's breezes that blew them this way and that, the softness of each girl's blossoming cushioning her laughter. Together, they lured us to the dances at the Kimball House and in Bar Harbor. One was a sylph, another a swan. One trapped you in the darkness of her eyes, another with the lightness of her step; and, just when your heart broke free another sprite appeared, her mouth turned downward at the edges, mocking your vain attempts at freedom as she ensnared you. They divided up their charms and used them recklessly, enslaving any boy they desired, taming their willing victim, then passing him along, one to the next, making the strongest giddy with the scent of their French perfumes—Givenchy, Chanel, Balenciaga—flora filled with rumors of ecstasy, essence of promises.

But our innocence was getting ready to move on. It no longer lived inside us. It was sidelined into riding shotgun, relegated to the seat we used to claim by the sudden burst of freedom that accompanied our drivers' licenses. Everything changed with the rush that came with driving in the dark. Route 3 was straight and empty late at night, and if your car could touch 90 it was the place to find that out, the place to race, the place to steal up, headlights off, upon another car that you then flashed and hurtled past, *Oh God I hope he didn't have a heart attack*, whoops of laughter, guttural cries of triumph, and the high pitched squeals of terror, the jittery girls, this once unnerved, exulting, all the rich and the glorious bright madness of touching seventeen. We had become knights on horseback and we learned to swagger some. We understood that our lunacy, though not meeting with approval, could earn a hot embrace.

It was early spring of my first senior year, after my aborted foray into public education at Lower Merion and my retreat into late night television. I suppose I had been allowed to come on the ski trip because it was my brothers' vacation and leaving me behind was not a real option. I suspect that there was some thought that getting me out of the house and having me do something I liked to do and be with people my age might help me to reengage with life. Skiing seemed much healthier than the all night movies, and no one seemed in a hurry to end the trip.

I awoke in stages. My mother said I spoke in French at first, which made her laugh since French was my worst subject. I didn't remember that, only the nurse hovering above me. She had short blond hair and when in focus swept my mind back to the dream. I had asked her to run off with

me—to let me show her just how much I knew about the world. When she demurred, I spoke more brutally, saying that I would force her if I had to. But then I had lost her in the eddying light.

The nurse wasn't there when I grew alert enough to know I that had not invented her. I could tell by the sound and touch of the sheets—there was solidity to the impression I could not will away—and by the pain when I tried to move, that although I was waking in an unfamiliar place, I had not so much escaped the real world as to have had it tumble over me. Everything had happened suddenly: the stomachache; my skiing down the mountain; the doctor at the medical building saying that I had appendicitis; the ride beside him in his car to the hospital; the hospital itself, Victorian, high-ceilinged, gray-walled with half a dozen beds; my mother saying "Yes" when told there wasn't enough time to have me flown to Denver; and the old man with the ether counting down from one hundred, the numbers rippling as if the voice had dropped them into a pool, just before they carried me off in waves into the darkness.

My blonde nurse came in; apparently she was glad to see that I was alive. I must have blushed. All business, she didn't notice. She came right up to me, gave me a "Welcome back!" smile, and asked me how I felt. I whispered, "Alright." My only other operation had been for tonsillitis, and I was expecting my throat to be sore again.

"Soon," she said, "you'll have to take a little walk."

Now I was not sure she was the same nurse who I had conquered in my dream. She looked the part, but nothing in her words or actions indicated that she had suffered from my abuse. I chose not to pry. The champion of my reverie best remained unrelated to my conscious self. If someone who resembled me had said the things I accused him of saying, he had escaped with the anesthesia. The boy recovering in the bed was too meek to speak of his more socially acceptable desires. As I watched the nurse checking the thermometer, I wondered if she was thinking about 98.6 or the twerp she had to take care of. I was not sure exactly what I had babbled, or even if she knew French. Perhaps my braggadocio had crumbled into some abject confession of my virginity and a desperate plea for her to make me a man.

The nurse showed me some pills, her manner pleasant but impersonal. She had become every girl I had ever wanted to take out and never found the courage to phone. Of course, this one was a girl no longer—most likely in her early twenties. In the dream that had made little difference, but in a world without hallucinations, it meant she was not even remotely accessible, even if I resumed the disguise of a swashbuckler.

It hurt to laugh, as I found out, and it hurt to cough. It hurt more to walk. And yet, I did all three. My mother and George came to visit, and my mother told me about having her appendix out when she was in Italy at a finishing school. She had been just my age and I tried to imagine her at seventeen in a bed like the one I was in. I could picture her propped at an angle and surrounded by nuns who knew no English and whose orders were for her to keep still for two weeks. Maybe this was how she had learned Italian. My lot seemed better. They brought me get-well cards and apologized whenever they said anything funny enough to make me wince with laughter.

Late in the afternoon I got a roommate, Jim, a super skier. Leg broken, cast up to his thigh, Jim wheeled himself in, claiming that the most painful thing was having to listen to them tear his Bogner pants to get them off. Something about the casual arrogance of his voice sounded familiar. I searched my mind and tried to pin it down. He waved as he went by the

foot of my bed and asked what my complaint was. I told him, and he said
he would trade places. I tried to smile. No, I had never seen him before.
He had the kind of clean-cut, magazine ad face I had always wanted to
trade mine in for.

In the hall, his girl was asking the doctor if she could come in. Before
he had time to answer, she was next to her Jim, her eyes filled with tears,
words tumbling from her mouth—Darling this and Darling that—promising she would be his private Florence Nightingale. Suzie was a wonderful
angel, blue-eyed and pert, kissing her wounded warrior as I lay stranded
behind *Life* four feet away. She was going to bring him anything he needed,
especially herself. Nothing was too much to ask of her, was what she said.

It was only after Suzie left and Jim had called up some friend on the
phone, explaining how he was taking her for a ride and joking about what
would happen when he ditched her, that I realized why I felt I had come
across him somewhere before. Jim was the protagonist of my dream, my
swaggering alter ego. Everything he said, every one of his gestures, provided more evidence that this was my phantom made flesh. He had escaped from my imagination only to come hobbling back to haunt me.

In some ways it was as if I had never awakened, as if I were he, and
what was left of me was merely a shadow that he cast. Certainly, whenever
Suzie came, they were oblivious to anyone else in the room. Even when
my mother and stepfather arrived, their lovemaking continued unabated,
unchecked by parental throat clearing and astonished laughter.

I lay there buried in my piles of reading material, absorbing Suzie sec-
ondhand. She flowed over me like the sea, washing every nook and cranny
of my body. She was the wind moaning through the trees in late November
or whispering in early August. I wanted to call out to her, scream that I
was on fire: Save me, save me! And when she left, there was the inevitable
phone call, the cynical, "She actually thinks she is going to marry me." I
thought of Hope at the dance and Mimi on the train. Not that I had promised them anything, not that I was as dishonest.

I left the hospital just three days after the operation. In four more I was
skiing again. There was a girl there who liked me very much, who had a
coke with me after we had finished our last run, whose hand I held while
watching Jailhouse Rock. I could tell she wanted to take the relationship a
good deal further, but each time I looked into her eyes, I thought of Suzie
and backed away, ashamed of my temptation to be Jim. I had no way of explaining to her what was holding me back, but in the morning I would tell
my cousin Brooke my stitches had come undone, which was actually true,
in hopes the message would be relayed, thinking that even if no one understood, I was going to banish the incubus who had promoted my conquests.

NEWPORT

Around and About My Father

about my father—
he was not
one to read
poetry

he liked to
cook, do things
with his hands, cut
flowers

fish, then eat
the fish with a
crisp white wine
chilled clean as

the crystal held
at the stem—
the roses an
abundant centerpiece

summer flowers—
for summer was his
season, its fullness
all he needed

around my father
the years grew
until the leaves turned the
gold of ripe peaches

and the bare trees
reminded him of times
his children
camped in branches

the first robin
would be drowned in
summer noises in
crickets ringing everywhere

their song his song
thickening the air like honeysuckle
his past storms
the forgotten storms of June

we drifted, carried the song
gliding across a bay
around and about
my father we curved

sailboats jibing at a mark
sent before a
freshening wind
sent beyond the bay.

For a couple of years, after our father sold Kent, our summer time with him was spent testing possible substitutes, such as Southampton, twice, and a cruise from Watch Hill up Buzzards Bay to Manchester. In the end, one stop on the cruise, Newport—where his friendships seemed to be deeper and where years before he had gone to the Naval War College and played at being an M.P.—became his second home.

We always approached Newport from the west. In those days that meant that we crossed Narragansett Bay by ferry. Once aboard, we became voyagers, the ten minutes crossing to the glittering town touched with anticipation. It was always summer, always a gentle breeze; we leaned over the rail to look at the bow wave and beyond it sailboats decorating the waters all the way out to the ocean. We were passing into another world, freed from the constraints we took for granted everywhere else, unfettered and fully in charge of ourselves. Returning to Newport each year was coming back to our spiritual home, the place where of all the places in our lives we felt we belonged.

Newport was our Eden. If we had eaten of the forbidden fruit, the fruit had induced forgetfulness because the Newport of the Belle Époque had not been rediscovered. Most of our friends there lived in Newport year round and looked upon us as stylish and urbane New Yorkers. This was a stunning development for me. I had thought of myself as on the periphery of the suave, the boy who hadn't known about button-down collars. By the time I came to Newport, I sported a veneer of sophistication that I did not have to think about. Besides, thinking in Newport was no more a requirement than working was. Like Northeast Harbor, Newport was a playground, though its cottages were Euro-palatial not New England shingled, and its summer people were more apt to be Texans than Philadelphians. We listened to Elvis and Cole Porter, we danced, we tennised, we laughed, we swam.

Our father with David, and me aboard the Moana.

I first saw Newport from a yacht my father had chartered one August. Splendid in her brightwork and her veneered mahogany, but too flat bottomed to be the least bit seaworthy, the Moana would putter about between ports of call where it was most at home. Inevitably, I longed for land the moment I left it. I am not quite sure why. Later, I would love sailing with my stepfather, especially in a bit of a sea, the rail under. But before that, harbors were more than havens to me. The sight of houses ringing the suddenly stilled waters was an elixir. Just the thought that we might soon be inside one of them was enough to get me talking for the first time in hours.

Wherever we went my father had friends who opened their doors to us. Ten minutes after setting foot on a dock, I would find myself sitting on the edge of a captain's chair or enfolded by the overstuffed down pillows of an impressive sofa. Even if our host was the most fearsome looking man, hair popping out of his ears, eyebrows on fire, I embraced him as my protector. In Newport this role fell to Mr. Cushing. He was almost tall enough to seem a giant to my ten-year-old mind, but I could tell he was a gentle one. After all, his hair had turned white as snow and his smile was wholehearted. Besides, he had a son near my age and a white clapboard house that went on forever and where I could quickly forget the relentless motion of the sea.

The Ledges was built on a point, and when the wind picked up, the ocean tried to lash at us from two sides. I loved the impotence of my recent nemesis. But there was much more to do than to sit about and feel smug about an enemy. The Cushings had sheep, which we tried to ride, and cliffs to climb on. We'd have a catch with Tomony Cushing, who was our age, on the lawn above a rock garden so lovely that I've spent many summers since on my own grounds trying to recapture the way the alyssum there spilled over the rocks and the saxifrage split the crannies. After dinnertime we'd head up to the third floor where we rummaged through a treasure trove of battered trumpets and old war uniforms. Let the winds howl: we could always build ourselves foxholes at the foot of our beds and settle into them to dream our dreams of glory.

Even for those who were used to it, swimming at Bailey's Beach in Newport always presented a challenge. A belt of crimson algae (not to be confused with red tide) girdled the gray sand. Those who had come from Southampton or the Vineyard were astonished. Where does this stuff come from? The seaweed was said to be a permanent legacy of the Hurricane of '38, a perpetual memorial to Mother Nature courtesy of herself; her way of reminding the wealthy that all the grandeur they could muster was still subject to the tides and the wind. The most dignified matron wading in the shadow of her splendid summer cottage had to emerge from the water peeling away the crab-like vegetation that clung to her pale skin like an unwanted child.

The only reason for any of us to enter the water and disturb the gulls that seemed very much at home there was to reach the raft floating enticingly beyond the seaweed. We were like a corps de ballet on point as we threaded our way through our local version of the Red Sea. "At least this crud could have been green," a visitor once said. "It looks like a featherbed some whale died bleeding on." No matter, we pressed forward and, after thirty steps or so, reassembled in the clear water on the other side. It was always an occasion to pause. Water up to our chests, we looked back to the cabanas, and to the substantial, symmetrical building that was the center of the beach club. It had been built to stand up to the next hurricane, and although the bricks had all been painted the same gray as the sand, the shutters were a desert tan, and the house retained the respectable solidity of a Jeffersonian mansion. On the beach itself our elders walked about, solemn and indecisive. We laughed at their posturing on the shoreline and imitated their cautious entries into the stew.

"Last one to the raft's a..."

"First one gets a date with—"

"Who cares?"

"Oh, sensitive."

We splashed our way seaward, careful to remain near the buoyed rope that led out to our destination. The horizon, which emerged reassuringly after each stroke, soon began to tip precariously. From the raft the people on the beach were rarely identifiable. Only someone like my father, whose bell shape was not disguised by distance, could be recognized. We all yelled or waved until we saw our target's tiny hand wave back, or until a friend pushed us back into the sea. Down we went, refusing to emerge until we had scooped a handful of sand off the bottom, soon to burst through the surface like proud porpoises, trying to splash the sunbathers.

Beachmound.

Sometimes it was important to rest out there. We lay on the raft and dried in the sun. I propped myself on my elbows and looked at the windows of the apartment my father kept in Beachmound, a converted mansion that overlooked the cove. It stood splendid in its whiteness, grand with Ionic columns and the patrician air of a Southern plantation. From my perch in the sea, I liked being able to see where I had arisen that morning and would go to sleep that night. It was as if the house were protecting us, a m'am'selle for the onset of adolescence. "Be careful," it seemed to call out. "Don't go any deeper."

No one ever looked forward to the swim back to shore. By the time we reached the seaweed we were tired and treaded water for a few minutes to recover. Inevitably, we spent those minutes yelling at the lifeguards, trying to convince them to launch a rescue boat and row out to where we were, sparing us from having to negotiate the stringy bands of weeds soon to be a second skin. But the lifeguards knew our tricks and only responded when the sea was rough enough to make the trip exciting. Otherwise, they stood beside their tower and grinned at our plight, ready to relish our struggle.

When we finally hit the beach, we came out sprinting and the momentum carried us all the way to the shower. There, someone not brave enough to have swum to the raft would tell us we had missed one of the Taylors in a two-piece bathing suit, and that we had also missed Mr. Elkins telling her it was not acceptable. We were supposed to admit our little informer into our group as a reward for his gossip, but it was hard to forgive him for his cowardice. After all, we were picking the weeds off our legs and he had visions of a near naked girl to mark the afternoon.

Half an hour later we were all laughing about it in our club-like space at The Studio. Next we practiced swearing on the tape recorder (a relatively new invention) or placed a prank phone call.

"Hello, this is WNPT, 690 on your radio dial..."

"Yes..."

"You probably know we have a weekly contest to see who wins our all expenses paid trip to Acapulco."

"Oh! Oh! Oh!"

"You could be the one, Mrs. Carmen."

"Oh! What do I have to do?"

"Just answer our simple question."

"Oh, I hope I can."

"Oh, I hope so, too, Mrs. Carmen. All of us down here at WNPT are rooting for you."

"Thank you."

"You are welcome, Mrs. Carmen. Now for the question."

"Oh!"

"Are you ready, Mrs. Carmen?"

"I think so!"

"How much wood would a woodchuck chuck if a woodchuck could chuck wood?"

Silence

"Mrs. Carmen, would you like us to repeat the question?"

"Oh, dear, could you?"

"I'm afraid not. Our time has run out. But we do have a consolation prize."

"Yes."

"Here it is…"

And we all gave the phone the raspberry before doubling up on the floor.

There were always five or six of us in The Studio: Tommy Cushing, Jimmy Lanier (my inspiration for ditching Hope Leonard at the junior cotillion), at least one of the Walker brothers, and my brother David and me. Tommy's grandfather had painted in it, but for years since then The Studio had become the domain of Tommy and his older brothers. His brothers were all away so it had become our playground (his sister Minnie was still too young to count). We spent at least part of every August trying to find the easiest ways to pass from our thirteenth to eighteenth summers in The Studio. It was the basement in Long Island elevated to a grand clubhouse—our sanctuary.

The room itself was spectacular, big as a small basketball court but without the empty spaces. Every few feet a Victorian loveseat or an art nouveau lamp resided. There were card tables, side tables, coffee tables, and settled in upon every one of them was an eclectic assortment of fig-urines from India or ashtrays from Dubai. You felt you were in the final resting place of the souvenirs of a world traveler who had been forbidden to bring his booty into the parlor.

High above us, gracing the upper reaches of the walls, framed depic-tions of benign aristocrats and their pretty sons and daughters kept watch. They had been portrayed in such a way that we found them the most permissive of guardians, endlessly pampering us with their tolerant eyes. Nothing we did, bawdy or cruel, raucous or repulsive, could get them to blink or raise an eyebrow. Perhaps having grown up in the late nineteenth or early twentieth century they might have delighted in our freedom, or maybe they just enjoyed the music we played at full blast over the elaborate hi-fi system. I like to think, in any case, that we entertained those captive spirits. It would be a shame if they missed out on the fun.

All the times there return to me as one. I know at first there were no girls, and that later on the tape recorder lost its charm, but still the days and nights play back as a single scene. The interruptions that took place between the visits live elsewhere. The blur of the years has allowed the sequence of events to wander off. What's left is a picture of Sybaris where space has usurped time, where what happened in The Studio has been transformed from a string of tenuously connected moments into an elaborate painting, like one of those huge canvasses filled with glimpses of all the artist's friends, each caught in a typical pose, part of an ensemble, a consort of Pan's children gathered in a celebration of the season.

A few of the girls, like Malley Richmond and Meade Bridges, were present almost from the beginning, more of a part of Newport than we were, girls who would go to a movie with us (I remember *Gigi* and *I Was a Teenage Werewolf*). Other kids came from everywhere in different shapes and sizes to The Studio. Some would strut into the place with bravado and arrogance; others would scurry about like mice, searching for the right piece of furniture to hide behind.

One memorable night a grouping in the middle of the room over-shadows both types. Joan Reeves has just said something that has made her admirers laugh. You can tell they are her admirers because they look at her breasts, so striking in their amplitude that you felt self-conscious even when you were not looking at them. Her friends, on the other hand, appear to be mildly shocked. One is glancing at the ceiling, another's mouth is halfway to a gape, and a third girl's tongue is on the verge of clucking. The friends stand side by side like the Three Graces in Bermuda shorts.

Far to their right a poker game is in progress. Many of the players' faces are indistinguishable from other countenances in the room—only here, between the deep puffs they take on their cigarettes, their expressions are universally serious, save for the unaffected smile of a smallish boy who is gathering in some chips. All the players are wearing Lacoste polo shirts. Each sports a different color, so that as individuals they give the impression of being fragments of a solemn rainbow. The light that suffuses the room from the windows on all sides suggests it is a cloudy day, which explains why the dancers over near the door on the left are indecipherable. It is the summer of "Blue Suede Shoes." No two couples are doing the same step. The Grace who had been staring at the ceiling has wrapped herself around the shorter winner of the poker game. Joan Reeves is doing something on her own and her partner appears half a beat behind her. Near them on a couch someone is asleep, a beer can in his hand. It's me.

"Wake up! Wake up! Time to go home!"

"What time is it?"

"It's late."

"Oh, God. Dad will kill us!"

"Not if we go now."

"Why's that?"

"Because he'll probably still be out himself."

"I don't know if I can ride my bike."

"Had a little too much?"

"It doesn't have a light on it."

"So what? The moon is out."

As soon as we step outside we smell the salt air. We stand suspended in the suddenness of the change from the smoky room. I shiver, though it is a warm night. Maybe I am thinking about the sailor who had trapped me the week before and tried to lure me away from going to Hope Leonard's house. Almost scared me from ever riding my bike again, at least in the dark, certainly through town.

"Come on, let's go," David tells me, and the two of us pedal up the short incline and then begin to gather speed as we slide down the Cushings' driveway. We both know the trick is on the turn into the main road. If no cars are coming, then we can swing wide without braking and hurtle down the road past the marsh and the beach club halfway up the hill on the other side only a few hundred feet from home.

Though we are only a foot apart, we are not racing. Intent on keeping our balance, we speak of nothing. The faint images and the wind rushing at us are sensed but not translated into meaning. The road flashes underneath us, we leave the cabanas behind and pass the tennis courts. We register all this and ignore it. Only when we are almost home and have slipped off our bikes to lessen the noise on the gravel, do we brothers dare to let the impressions of our environment stir our imaginations.

By the time we reach the front door, the two-minute trip has taken on heroic overtones. It has been a wartime dash through enemy lines. The barely noticed landscape now fills with ghosts. Trees crawl with snipers; the road is dotted with mines. It took a lot of skill and a bit of luck just to make it this far. We had been entrusted with a message for the general, and as we open the door to the headquarters, we stand tall and prepare to salute.

In truth, we are delighted to find that no one is in. The report can wait until morning. A minute after entering our apartment, we are in bed and the light is out. It is safe to dream some more. Perhaps it isn't wartime. Perhaps it is a hundred years ago and we were galloping by Cochise to get a message to the cavalry. No, that's not it. Wrong country. Wrong time, too. Medieval England, then. A knight and his squire capturing the grail, returning to our king to receive his blessing. Trumpets salute us. "You have done well," the monarch says. "I'll grant you immortality."

In the morning our father rises first. I hear the water running in the kitchen and tell David to wake up. Neither of us wants to move, but we do. We want to help and know that our help is wanted. I stumble toward the bathroom to splash some water on my face. Even in this state, I am able to think ahead to what the day will bring. Somehow, I know it is Sunday and that means breakfast will be eggs and bacon. I'll make the juice, David the toast. We'll eat, the three of us crowded around the small table in the kitchen. Between bites, my father will ask us about the night before, and we will tell him who we saw and much of what we did, but claim we were home half an hour before we were. Afterward, we will wash the dishes and police our room, knowing that by ten we will have to pass inspection. Then we'll be free to go on down to Bailey's, play tennis, swim, have lunch, take in a movie if it rains, or return to The Studio.

But it is important to pause at breakfast and its dynamic, the interaction between the three of us, the chance for David and me to sit on either side of the small round table, our father between us, a family. Somehow I sensed that this was what family was, a chance to feel connected, a mass I could relate to, communion consummated in the shared enjoyment of eggs and bacon and white toast. My mother always had breakfast in bed. And we rarely went to find her as we did our grandmother, who seemed such a morning hostess to us. Our father chose to eat with us, to talk with us, to listen to our prattle. We loved that he seemed to make us so much a part of his life for whole weeks at a time.

When we returned to our Philadelphia home, we never talked of breakfast, only of the extraordinary freedom we were permitted in Newport, a freedom we knew was not appreciated, but which we celebrated because it meant we were trusted, a trust we believed we had earned at the breakfast table, washing the dishes, policing our rooms, and being courteous to our elders.

After breakfast I studied my image in the mirror and tried to make my chin more prominent. There seemed to be a pimple forming near my nose. The sun had flooded my face with freckles. I searched for a consoling platitude. "Nothing is perfect" came to mind. After all, I remembered, the seaweed was waiting for me at the beach.

Newport in the mid-fifties was just beginning to recover from several decades of neglect. Many of the magnificent summer cottages, trophies of the Gilded Age, were empty. A few, like Beachmound, were being converted into apartments; the grandest and least habitable were opening their doors as museums; a couple, like The Elms, were graced each August by a dowager descendent of the original owners. A great deal of hope was being placed in Texans who enjoyed spending their money in more flamboyant ways than the Easterners who had come to their positions at least partly through inheritance and thought displaying their wealth was either ostentatious or too great a drain on their capital.

This Newport had no jazz festival. The older part of town was not yet gentrified. The brave had opened a few boutiques near the Casino, the fine McKim, Mead, and White shingle style building that fronted the Tennis Hall of Fame; but Bellevue Avenue was not Worth Avenue. And if Newport was not the ghost town it had been ten years earlier, the people in it who lived the most grandly seemed somewhat secretive about it, as if they wanted the world to focus on what had been lost so they could live on islands less visible than the monumental Breakers. Their excesses were protected from view by the century-old trees, fully matured so that even the grandest of the houses knew shade, and passersby would barely notice that the paint glimpsed between the purple leaves of an elegant copper beach was peeling.

Besides, the pleasures shared by my father's friends were often simple pleasures: Romeo y Juileta #1s, Romanée-Conti, libraries of rare erotica, golf, the grass courts at the Casino, picnics on Gooseberry Island. Those who lived in splendor did so unassumingly and looked upon the young with benign expressions. They enjoyed our laughter, how at ease we were traipsing through their world. We were spirited, but not rebellious. We took privilege for granted for it was what we knew, an addictive soporific that protected us. We may have been decorative appendages but we were the center of our circumscribed worlds, and because we rarely ventured out, we had little idea anything beyond us mattered. There were not many of us so we were somewhat in demand. For a resort town, Newport at the time was under populated. The central event of the summer was the tennis tournament on the Casino's courts where the best players in the world— Australians Laver, Rosewall, and Emerson; Americans Trabert and Seixas—all classified as amateurs at the time, came to play and be hosted by the gentry. Even here, we counted for something. Once I ended up not as a ball boy, but as a linesman in a quarterfinal match. I remember blowing a call and being stared at, but it was worth it, because it gave me a certain caché with a girl I was desperate to flirt with.

That must have been after I had gotten my license. Time then changed the routine a little. My father's good friends the Strawbridges had taken the apartment next to ours. Pandy, about my age, who I had known off and on for years, had become my closest friend. On a typical afternoon it was usually possible to find us sitting around in one of our living rooms and talking about the world between bites of the buttery roast beef tea sandwiches the maid had brought us. I sipped a gin and tonic. It was most likely a weekend—I had a summer job somewhere. Pandy was often telling me that I should take myself more seriously and put aside the clownish make up that helped me entertain the world. I reddened, past embarrassments coursing through my mind. But the words were always spoken gently, and I agreed with them.

It was hard not to agree with anything Pandy said because nothing about her struck me as being selfish. Besides, there was never any edge to her voice. Not that it was low or soothing. It was simply that there was no shriek in even the highest notes. The force behind whatever she said was packaged in down.

"You mean I am fat," she said.

"No, if anyone is, it's me."

She smiled. Her face was round and when she smiled I thought of a balloon with eyes, nose, and a mouth sketched on it. A red balloon, because she had such color in her cheeks.

I let it pass and instead went on about myself. I wanted her to know that there was every bit as much to me as she seemed willing to believe. But we were not in love. If our hands brushed together, there was no sudden pounding of the heart. Pandy gave me entrees to her friends and shared an occasional secret. After years of wondering what it would be like, I realized suddenly one day that I had found a sister. (Sydney, my actual sister, who has since come to play the part very well, was two at the time.)

The sun streamed through the windows. The dust particles basked in the brightness miming the indolent women lounging at Bailey's Beach, which we could see through the windows. Beyond Bailey's on a hill sat The Ledges. I wondered who was in The Studio. Pandy and I talked about our childhoods, and about how parts of the past could suddenly reappear unexpectedly, in the echo of a long forgotten sound or in a scent that had been lost for years.

"Do you know," I asked her, "that the lobby of the Ritz in Boston smells just like the yacht Daddy used to charter? When he came to me at school, he always stayed there, and as soon as I walked into the lobby I'd be tied up to the dock right here in Newport."

As if on cue, my father's footsteps announced his approach up the stairs. There was no hurry to them. He walked as he drove these days, leisurely, savoring the new vista brought on by even the slightest motion. I told Pandy that sometimes it seemed we were only floating toward the future or lazily punting ourselves down some canal in Shangri La.

"Or being punted," she added, as Mary brought in the last of the tea sandwiches.

Both of her parents and my father were almost old enough to have grandchildren our age. They were of Seebee and Aunt Isabel's generation and they seemed to enjoy us at that time with the kind of unalloyed pleasure Abraham must have had with Isaac. Not that we thought of them as distant figures from another age. No, we emulated what we treasured in them, vying to see which one of us could be the most unhurried.

It was almost evening. Mr. Strawbridge strolled about his living room in a glorious silk bathrobe having just returned from a swim. A cigar jutted from his mouth; despite its lack of line, it looked elegant. The lines around his eyes belied his dour countenance. He made a wry remark about the pace of our existence.

"Bobby, Bobby!" a voice chirped from behind a door. Mrs. Strawbridge asked her husband if he knew that they were due in fifteen minutes at the Fraziers.

"Mmmmmm...." he said, and took another puff on his cigar.

Soon his wife emerged, her dress rustling, her jewels bedazzling. He fixed his Florence a drink and then transported him and his cigar into the bedroom.

My father appeared next, bringing some roses in from the garden. His dinner was not until later and he hadn't yet changed.

"Oh, look at those! How lovely, Eddie," Mrs. Strawbridge said. And my father, accepting her offer of a drink as his reward, joined us.

When Mrs. Strawbridge died some fifteen years or so later, I sat down to write Pandy a letter, even though I had not seen her in a long time. I wanted to tell her how I had felt when my father died, especially about the time a few months after his death when I had returned to Newport. It had been mid-fall and the leaves were turning, something I did not associate with my summer home. That helped in a way, letting me see a different world and notice for the first time how remarkable the great oaks and beeches of the Vanderbilts and the Fishes had become. They were statelier than any of the mansions they overshadowed and, crowned with brilliant gold and reds, they held dominion over the deserted grounds and avenues, great rulers in their prime. But back in the apartment, at night, when there was nothing to look upon but the familiar lamps and tables, memories invaded.

Each chair, each picture on the wall, and even the small portable television hidden in the corner of the room brought back to me the image of my father. His absence seemed so tangible, as easy to feel as the carpet I lay upon. I reached out for him in grief, hoping my tears would have the power to produce a new Lazarus. I sputtered out his name, "Daddy, Daddy," my voice a child's again, my heart desperate to believe my words had the power of incarnation, to summon back the look he gave me and Mike Meehan as we lounged in the living room before a party, our black ties loose about our necks, celebrating the enormous gin and tonics courtesy of him and the huge Stueben glasses we had poured them into. "You are planning to make the dinner?" he asked. We laughed. We were. We did.

But it was only memory. I was not even granted a vision of him in his new transparency. Later I dried my face with my sleeve and stared at the ceiling, wondering what to do in a whimpering conversation with myself. I kept saying he was welcome back in any guise, whether to lecture me for disposing of his clothes, or to be disappointed at the dishes left in the sink. I wanted him to walk into the room and shout at me for not writing him for two months. "But, but..." I'd stutter, wanting to explain. Of course, he would understand, and I would be careful to be very still, making no sudden movements, fearing that surprise might set off another heart attack.

"Dear Pandy," I began. "So many years..."

How young I had been! Twenty-one. I told her how, after the early bursts of grief had passed, I had come to see my father once again strolling between the two apartments. Her mother was always there, bringing a smile to my face with her full and unrestricted laugh, the air dancing in the pleasure she took in everything she saw—the purple in the clouds beside the setting sun, her pretty daughter's pretty dress, how its color matched the roses in the Meissen vase.

I wanted Pandy to know the way I had seen her mother; to see I had never forgotten all the kindnesses she had shown me. I understood my life was richer for the pleasure that she gave me and I was not ashamed for having taken it, for having spent so many August afternoons languishing in luxury.

Somehow I never sent her the letter. It sat in a drawer for weeks just like the letters that I had had to write at school that never left my bureau. Then I had been too lazy to go and buy a stamp. Now I was puzzled and unsure. Scared, perhaps, of sounding overly trite, or just wanting to leave the times that I had remembered undisturbed and instead letting them resurface unblemished in dreams.

Newport is very different today. Eisenhower, when he was president, took his vacation in Newport and helped start its reawakening. I remember getting out of a car and watching him hit a six iron on a par three at the Newport Country Club, a hole that I had once shot an eight on. Men with guns in their golf bags stood on an adjacent green. That was before the America's Cup, which would do more than the Jazz and Folk Festivals to beckon the glitterati and reawaken a sleepy town. The homes along Thames Street have changed from shanties into handsome townhouses. The Elms, where Pandy's Aunt Julia resided, is now a museum, but some of the lesser "cottages" have rediscovered splendor. The seaweed alone remains unchanged, purpling the shore.

I've returned from time to time and looked up at the portico of our old house. I can still hear the voices of my father and his friends.

"Oh, look at those. How lovely, Eddie!"

"Time to police your room. Now you're cooking on the front burner…"

"This is station WNPT…"

But the rest of the transmission no longer comes back to me. Someone told me a few years ago that the Strawbridges had actually bought Beachmound and that it has since become Pandy's. Her son was married there in the late nineties. It still looks the same. Some turn, some do not.

Eddie, sitting on the porch of The Ledges, having brought a Jereboam of Louis Roederer to celebrate what could have been his July 4th birthday.

Dancing with Brooke when I was eighteen at a party Seebee gave for her at The Sycamores. This is how I usually looked when Melzie saw me.

MELZIE

It was Nicole who called to tell me. The news was very bad. What with the brain damage, it was best if Melzie died. That's what the doctors said. And we said it, too, back and forth as consolation.

I had known Nicole since I had been three. I remember playing in her bed at nine. She was to be the designated romance of my childhood. Whenever I spoke to her on the phone and her face was not there to distract me, my mind wandered through her house as I had frequented it so many years before, exploring the cramped staircase off the kitchen, climbing up to the bathroom next to her room, finding my way past the nurse's nightgown hanging on a hook, to my friend, who seemed surprised that I had come to her from that direction. After all, the door to my room was only a few feet from hers. But I loved her house, its maze of small rooms and unexplored passages, and when I set off to find her, I wanted an adventure. I wanted to be Theseus finding the end of the maze.

Nicole's voice sounded so distant that at first I thought it was a bad connection. Then, as she went on and I realized what she was telling me—that Melzie had fallen from a horse, she was in a coma, there had been damage to her brain... she had had no business going off like that riding on her own, she should have known better and been more careful—I understood that the distance in Nicole's voice was taking the place of tears.

The funeral was in Washington. I didn't go. Death happened to old pets and grandmothers and not to anyone I knew. I made up an excuse. Nicole said she understood. I tried to picture her in her house, tried to bring back the stairway off the kitchen. Instead of watching Melzie crash, I would find the miniature dollhouse Nicole had hidden beneath the covers. I would think of Alphonso, the du Pont's butler, and the time he had taken me to a Negro League baseball game and had convinced me that Josh Gibson had hit balls harder and farther than Hoot Gibson had ever dreamed of, and that Satchel Paige could strike out my hero every time he faced him. "Every time?" I had asked. "Well, maybe not every time," Alphonso laughed.

Later, I heard the funeral was a mess, and that after the service the mourners my age went to the Hardins' house and drank themselves into stupors. I didn't want to hear the stories of that time, but they became so much a part of me that I would later turn scenes from them into fiction, writing about a pretty blonde girl who had gone to weep but ended up sick in the toilet.

Maybe it wasn't the Hardins' house. Maybe, though, that was where I had first met Melzie, two years before on a drunken New Year's Eve. I would wonder about that when, the following December, I saw her at a dinner dance. She walked right up to me and asked me how I had been. I said "great," and tried to place her face, amazed that I couldn't. Nothing about it seemed familiar, though it was hard to imagine that I could have forgotten anyone so pretty or direct. But clearly I had. I looked down at the bourbon and ginger ale in my glass and looked at her again. Perhaps she had lost some weight. Perhaps she had worn enough makeup to hide her freckles. Perhaps the room had been dark. Perhaps she had spent most of the night wrapped in some boyfriend's arms. I offered to get her a drink.

"Remember, I don't drink," she said.

I did drink, though not as much as I once had. I had vomited in the Grand Canal in Venice and sworn never to be sick that way again.

"Or smoke," she added, as I offered her a Camel.

It should have been an awkward moment, but I was smitten.

That night, I danced with Melzie half a dozen times, and when I wasn't with her I was watching her, catching the way she moved past me, her eyes brighter than the chandeliers, her laugh light as the puff pastry at Le Pavillon.

Who was the party for? They were always the same—champagne and pink tablecloths, necklaces, and music. It made no difference whether we whirled and sipped and supped and two stepped underneath the pale blue canvas of a sumptuous tent that stretched across a proud father's once prized lawn or in a gilded hotel ballroom replete with sconces and balconies and murals and velvet-cushioned chairs. The music was always the same (though the connoisseurs among us would swear that Lester Lanin could not hold a candle to Meyer Davis): show tunes, Cole Porter and Rogers and Hart, a high society take on jazz, Basie with violins. All of it was great to dance to, to forget the Durhams and all the precious steps you learned, and to think you were Fred Astaire. The revelers never changed, either, whether we showed up in New York or Wilmington, Southampton or Bryn Mawr. Everyone had known each other from prep school or Palm Beach, Fisher's Island or Piping Rock. Each debut was a reunion.

It was important to take it all in stride, to display a kind of nonchalant acceptance of the thousands spent on us. We knew the premise was absurd—the girls whose year it was for "coming out" had been out making the scene for years already. But how else were we to spend our time on vacation? Parties were the birthright of the young. Why question their existence? Nothing is more graceless than turning down a gift, and nothing was admired more than grace.

How was Melzie dressed? Simply, I suppose, in blue to match her eyes, a blue would always go so nicely with the color of her hair, a strawberry blonde—more strawberry than blonde. I told her that the horse I had ridden in Wyoming was a roan, and she pretended I had insulted her. Our conversation went no deeper then. I did not want to risk claiming to be an artist who wanted to paint her in the nude, though I was tempted. And I wasn't about to slip into something more serious when I was afraid a frown would scare her off, or cause her to frown back at me, a butterfly trapped by a spider. No, it was better to trust to Cole Porter than to drop names selected from my college catalogue. Porter's melodies could keep us in a paradise my monotone could only sabotage.

> *In the mountain greenery*
> *Where God made the scenery*

A long way from the sprigs of holly that served as a decoration, but the lyrics took us there, and we talked for a moment about sunsets, and we tried to take it deeper.

Then a hand on my shoulder predicted that someone not so different from me was cutting in to take my place. I stepped aside and watched my angel glide away until she had vanished with her new partner into the mass of other dancers.

The next time I saw Melzie was at Nicole's house, about a week after the dance. I was on my way back to college and had stopped off to see my childhood sweetheart before I left.

"Guess who's here," she teased, and when I shrugged my answer, she mouthed, "Melzie."

And so she was, and she was just as I remembered, despite the change of costume. Nicole was playing Cupid, and showering me with arrows. She obviously relished her role despite the thickness of my skin. "I hardly know this girl," I thought. "Besides, I've already decided to be in love with someone else."

Still, I stayed longer than I had planned and spent the night, missing a freshman psychology test the next morning. When I finally left, I did not want to go. I needed more time. A chance to take Melzie's pulse and find out if she was real.

Driving south, I was not sure. She had a beauty that seemed to fly against my sensual dreams: pale and unearthly, her skin too delicate, her profile too sharp; her azure eyes as lovely as Mrs. Snowden's morning glories, but so large they seemed to bend under their own weight. She struck me as belonging to another century, at home in this one only when she danced—strained by a world without music and the illusions of a ball. I didn't understand why she had come so close to me, as if she had leaped out of some early Renaissance fresco, one of Botticelli's maidens who noticed I was staring at her face and decided to find out why I was so rude.

What had we talked about? Next to nothing. Just enough to pass the time without too many pauses. I had been careful not to laugh too loudly or coarsely. Surely anything too clumsy would have frightened her away. I had spent so much of my youth retreating into the guise of a clown, and I knew that with Melzie I needed to resist the temptation. She was no closer than the time before, just more familiar. I had been allowed the chance to study her high cheekbones and to guess that if I ever kissed her it would be a romantic moment but not a carnal one, her lips soft as the carnation petals in the vase next to my bed at Nicole's.

When I got back to college I didn't write her. I was afraid she would not answer, and strand a part of my heart three hundred miles away. Anyway, I hadn't much to say. Beyond "Dear Melzie" very little came. I could not afford to risk appearing foolish. I imagined her puzzled by my words, showing them to some strange boy or girl who would laugh derisively. That cackle pinned me to the wall, leaving me to dry out like some specimen moth in a display case. I heard it every time I tried to think up my first sentence. I was a fool afraid of appearing foolish. It occurred to me I might send a postcard—something funny, a card on which naked Bacchus rode astride a turtle. I still had one from the summer before, picked up along with a leather belt in Florence. The risk was that she might see me in the paunchy god, and I would be forever locked within his image.

Though there had been times I had played such a part, this was not one of them. I was determined to wean myself away from my dependency on the frivolous. I wanted to be taken seriously, but how could I ask this girl who had never heard me talk about the soul or D.H. Lawrence think of me as more than a fop, Beau Brummell without style, a comic crippled with the disease of insincerity? She had never seen me without my foils, and I was not about to change them. That would take a kind of nerve I knew I did not possess.

And then she had always seemed to me so insubstantial, a dryad vanished behind a tree, a sprite turned into ether. I needed someone who I sensed was made of baser stuff. Whoever judged me ought to share mortality with me, at the least. How could she understand the kind of pain I felt stumbling down the stairs? She was so clearly from another sphere. But none of that seemed to matter very much when I saw her again.

It was the following summer, in Newport. During the week I was working in New York in the mailroom at CBS. It was my first real job: $56 a week. On Saturdays and Sundays I was in Rhode Island offering highlights of the city to all who would listen. One Saturday proved to be no exception. Nursing a gin and tonic by the bar at Bailey's, I was rambling on about how Johnny Finger danced the twist groin grinding with a girl at Coney Island.

"Come on!" a doubter interrupted after I announced he had had a red handkerchief decorating his open fly.

"No, really. I believe it," I went on. "He and this other guy, the Greek, have the nerve to do anything. You should have seen the deck of cards Aristo brought in. You know, he slips one of these things in with the regular mail and gives it to a secretary he thought would appreciate the entertainment. The best one he called a full house; it..."

I sensed a new listener standing behind me. I hesitated, turned to look over my shoulder.

"Melzie..."

"Don't let me interrupt..."

"How are you?"

"Great."

"Can I get you a drink?"

"Remember, I don't drink."

"A lemonade. They have great lemonade."

"I'd love one."

My story never had an ending.

I didn't care if Melzie didn't drink, didn't smoke, but I did care that at Nicole's she had also added, "I also don't kiss boys." I asked her if any of her proclamations had undergone a change.

"No."

"I had hoped you would say, 'Not yet.'"

"Not yet, not never."

"'Not never'—that's a double negative. Sounds promising."

"To you, I promise nothing."

"Not even a dance tonight?"

"Oh, that I'll promise you."

I felt the game of tennis I had played that morning was on again, only now I was swatting words instead of balls. They went and they came back, they went and they came back. Always kept in play because neither of wanted to hit a winner and end the rally.

Then she was called away. I wanted her to stay, ask her to practice serving, but wasn't quick enough to find the words that would keep her.

"Until tonight," I said, feeling I had double faulted.

"Until tonight."

Melzie had come to Newport for the dance of a classmate. Her summer had been spent travelling from one spa to another. I tried to imagine her in a car bumping its way from Watch Hill to Saratoga. I couldn't. I decided that she must have arrived by glider, easing in from Amagansett. What difference did it make if she were only visiting the earth? I had her in my arms and she was raising no objection, was even smiling, following my every step without the slightest hesitation. It was like dancing with Terpsichore herself, as if the muse had freed me from my routine awkwardness. Around and around we went, spinning tops, darting past surprised and stolid couples, paired gazelles slipping through a herd of buffaloes. We were swept up by the music until we were the music. Even when I sang the words the spell refused to dissipate.

Just one of those things
Just one of those fabulous flings

And in the morning she remembered me, remembered that she had agreed to see me in New York one night later in the week.

Melzie came with me to my six o'clock class at Columbia. It was my chance to show her that there was more to me than banter and pirouettes. I may have been shallow, but my shallowness was complex. If I was a sybarite, I was someone who had come to college to read and to think. That I loved to be perceived as someone who loved to read and to think was also true. If I enjoyed the music I heard as a subscriber to a chamber series at The Peabody Conservatory, I also enjoyed being seen as someone who could engage with a Bartok quartet. I wanted to be able to understand Sartre and Merleau-Ponty at least in part so my peers might believe I understood.

I was inauthentic but I could argue that it was impossible to escape from inauthenticity. The best we could do was to be honest about the role we chose to play.

Not that I dared to speak in Metaphysics 204; understanding nods served me better than garbled interjections. I hoped she could stay awake. The philosophical implications of Heisenberg's principle are pretty soporific to the non-elect. This was an early day on my journey to intellectual sophistication. I may have had a faint grasp of what was going on, but any attempt to articulate my ideas would have exposed me as a charlatan.

I sat up in the desk chair trying to forget the heat, wanting to look studious. The professor was making a point about Gilbert Ryle, and I made a cryptic rune in my notebook, more for Melzie's benefit than for my own. Whenever possible I looked at her to make sure she hadn't bolted from the room. Now and then she'd give me a puzzled look and I would try to indicate that I sympathized by rolling my eyes. Otherwise, she simply sat gracefully and looked politely at the speaker. I felt like writing her an apology, explaining why I had put her through this ordeal, telling her how wonderful she looked, the Queen Anne's lace, the daisies in a field of wildflowers blooming in the desert of Hamilton Hall. How fresh she was, cool in the shimmering heat, rescuing me from the high, barren, and long unpainted walls of Room 205.

When it was over and I unstuck myself from my chair, she rose and I wanted to take her hand and close my eyes and be wafted back to Kent in the summertime. We could play down by the brook until dark. She could be a nymph glistening in the water, and I could simple sit there mute with admiration.

Instead we grabbed a bite to eat and then went back to the apartment she was staying in. I was nervous in the elevator, realizing I was in the same building I had visited six weeks before. The lure that time had been Ellen, a girl I'd discovered at a party who seemed to find the bushes out behind the tent more interesting than the dance floor. What would she say if she could find me now, more captivated by a rival's glance than all the jewels she had to offer?

I understood the ground rules for the night. I was permitted to hold my Melzie's hand. I looked at her wondering what it was that made her seem so far away. Perhaps she had been alive for five hundred years, and if I came too close her skin would start to crack, her face might recede back into that Botticelli fresco from which she had escaped. Then I could tell her that I had discovered her secret but would always keep it safe. What was it anyway? Had someone hurt her once and left her broken like the glasses I had dropped? Or did she have mysterious liaisons with a famous diplomat, perhaps—wasn't she a diplomat's daughter? But I didn't think that was probable. More likely she had imbibed a potion once formulated by Diana to save the honor of her worshippers.

Oh, well, I knew she liked me, and if we were playing a game, clearly she was winning. I suspected she simply didn't trust me, something I could not argue with, as I really was untrustworthy. I sat beside her, tacitly accepting the position she gave me, without complaint or question, securely in her thrall.

I talked about my job, but did not pick up where I had left off mid-story in Newport a few days before. No, I talked about how interesting it was. Not the climbing up and down the twenty-one flights of stairs to deliver packets of letters, bills, packages, inter-office mail, and telegrams to people who controlled the news and entertainment of the world—though I supposed I was proud of how hard the work could be at times. No, I talked about my cohorts, how they had not begrudged me, and the boy from Greenwich whom they saw as a clone of mine, with our summer jobs, on our college track.

Most of them were my age or slightly older, all from New York, more Brooklyn and Queens than Manhattan, products of a school system they described as worthless—teachers with feet on their desks reading the Daily News, waiting to retire. All of my coworkers were intelligent and most were ambitious, though one of us did want to become an elevator operator because of the union benefits. As a group we formed a kind of mini U.N. and laughed about our varied alliances: Anglo-German, Greco-Roman, African-Lebanese, Israeli-Indian. We were all proficient in firing rubber bands like missiles. Each of us took pride in where he came from, but I was amazed at how easily we got along.

I told Melzie how it gave me hope for the world. I recalled for her a moment one morning when the air raid sirens had gone off—none of us had heard about a drill—and we had all frozen, thinking that the nukes were headed out way and we would be spending our last minutes together. I then ruined it by telling Melzie that, of course, I would have rather spent those minutes with her. She shook her head and laughed. Had she ever met anyone as transparent as me? She refused to answer that question.

The last time I saw Melzie was over Labor Day Weekend. I drove out to Southampton in my first car, a new Ford Falcon that my father, mother, and grandmother had given me for making it to twenty. It was no flashy roadster but a kind of equivalent to Don Quixote's Rocinante, and it was enough to blot out the pain of having failed my first two driver's tests three years before. I saw it as turning me from a squire into a knight despite its black exterior and gray bench seats.

I was so impressed with my new sense of self-importance that I neglected road signs and found that I was lost somewhere north of Riverdale. When I finally arrived at my friend Mike Meehan's house more than an hour late I was jeered. Full of bluster, I came in swearing at the road signs, claiming that the idiot who had put them up was either drunk or had relationships with sheep. I had to have a drink. I made one, put my feet up on a wicker table, took them off when Mrs. Meehan entered, stood, turned charming for the moment, and when she left slipped back into vulgarity.

That night was Marcia Meehan's party. Melzie was there, but so was someone else, a girl who'd been a child two summers before when I had engaged in a beer drinking contest with my old pals Meehan and McKnight from the Valley Ranch. Now she was anxious to prove to me how much she had changed. Still, even on the grass behind the tent I thought of Melzie as my Dulcinea. Why wouldn't she come stare at the stars with me? Hear me whisper the names of the constellations? She knew me better than this girl; she liked me more.

I never had an answer, and the next night I was Melzie's escort and I tried to win her with body, brain, and telepathy. When I danced with her, I tried to disrupt the flow. I talked incessantly and ridiculed her litany of principles. I almost asked if she had noticed me slip outside with my new friend. See what you have driven me to do? See how you have turned a devoted cavalier into a tawdry brute?

Dear Melzie, I was too young to pay you proper court. I didn't know enough to see you as a young princess who had had medieval schooling. I didn't think I had the time to have the patience you demanded. You carried love within your eyes, filled with confused adoration. I was but a jester, and no matter how hard I tried to let my guise go, it crept up again.

But her eyes were still enough to hold me near. At dawn I drove her back to the house where she was staying. I scrambled from the car and raced to open the door for her. The sun was rising and beside it was the morning star. I walked Melzie up some steps and stood with her for a second at the door. I said I hoped she had not found me cranky and thanked her for her tolerance. She laughed, gently, lifting my heart enough for me to kiss her forehead softly.

"I don't kiss boys," she said.

"I know," I said, "but I kiss girls and you're a wonderful girl."

I turned, feeling as gallant as Sir Galahad. The sun was higher now and the star had disappeared. I went down the steps and looked back to wave. Melzie was halfway in the door, but she smiled and waved back.

Nicole's call came less than two weeks later. I remember hanging up the phone and sitting on the bed. I wondered if Melzie had been frightened. I tried to think of how I felt when the roan Jake tripped and sent me plummeting. It seemed to be that I had been more scared sailing at night with my stepfather. There had been a wave that looked to me like death approaching from the starboard quarter. Seeing it made me shiver, but I hadn't cried.

At first I told myself that she had not meant that much to me, as though that thought would help me not to think constantly about what happened. Then, too, by shying from her funeral, I had saved myself from seeing her in the ground. That was important. After all she had never struck me as having any weight. She was a firefly and had flown heavenward. What was there to mourn in that? Her natural environment was hardly here, certainly not closed off in some cramped study sealed from the sky forever. She had been no more to me than a winning character from a historical romance. A celebrated maid set in the court of Eleanor of Aquitaine. She would appear again. I would find her in that painting, or catch her waving to me, her figure caught by the light and more brilliant than the newly risen sun, there, from a half opened door.

But every time I raised my head and dreamed, my heart quickening, that she was here, I found myself staring at an empty wall. I wanted to see if her hair was as I remembered it, her eyes really that blue. I wanted to hear her speak again, my body turned into a harp, her words and gestures light fingers gracing the wires. She made me dance so beautifully, wove my awkwardness into glissandos.

Nothing. She wasn't there. She isn't here. There is no sound now beyond that of these fingers on the keys. It is hard to know what she meant to me at the time; our relationship had no depth. We were moths attracted to the flame, but such cautious moths. When she left it was if she had never been. But she took with her so much that was ephemeral at the time, the world I loved but was never serious about, a living in a present without an anchor, enjoyable, untainted by the desire to find meaning, a desire I let emerge from time to time, but elegantly disguised in rhetoric. I had spent so much of life enamored of surfaces. I was a pastiche of gestures, the deeply inhaled cigarette, the glass of champagne tilted with an extended pinky, the light banter, the intellectual veneer occasionally undermined by a deep streak of juvenile humor, which now and then I managed to exhibit humiliatingly in front of a dubious audience. At times it was hard for even me to take myself seriously, despite my metaphysics class (I had always loved the word metaphysics—it sounded so smart. Oddly none of my friends who went to the best schools ever sounded especially smart. They had no need to.) Perhaps when Melzie died I let go of the most foolish parts of myself. Or she took them with her. If Sartre was right and you mourn for the part of you that you gave the person who dies, then I must have mourned for the loss of that casual person I pretended I was.

Not so less than a year later, when my father died on that day I had gotten up to have breakfast with him. I remember being in my room when the phone rang. "Your father is very sick," the voice of his friend Charlie Burns said. I knew what the words meant and went to wake David who ended up having to identify his body at the morgue while I, the eldest, found myself sitting at his desk in his office.

We drifted through the next three days. Eddie was with my mother and George in Majorca, all scrambling for tickets to fly back. Fortunately, David and I were not completely alone. I was with Rosemary, who I had fallen in love with on a blind date a year and a half earlier, had courted relentlessly, and who I would marry in just over an year; and somehow Serena, daughter of my mother's best friend, came to be with David. Eleven days before, on my twenty first birthday, Serena and I had danced, and I had kissed her shamelessly under the stars when Minnie Cushing debuted at The Ledges.

Everything a blur. And two days later, the funeral. A full church. We are ushered in from the back. The memory still locked within me, I wrote:

> "A great tribute," the man of God
>   proclaimed. "Over six hundred people
>   and he wasn't even famous."
>
> Part of me still idles in the pew,
>   a child in suit and tie,
>   his tie, my eyes
>
> averted from the flag, seeking
>   solace in the candles, my mind
>   wavering within the nave,
>
> abandoning the mums for
>   flower girls, the grief
>   for lust, my father

for the blonde I chased
   along a beach
      three weeks before.

We lit candles, too,
   but moved with summer music,
      "The evening breeze. . . ."

She helps me dance his funeral,
   a shameless spin until the
      heat rescues my conscience

and I shrink onto the velvet cushion
   beyond assimilation. . . .
      The congregation joins the last amen;

a hymn begins— walk slowly, do not
   turn. Before the church
      a well protected hearse

reflects St. James' stones.
   Inside the ceaseless sifting of the cars,
      they rest and are not moving.

The other night I dreamed of Pandy and Nicole. It was the first time
I had seen them in many years. Melzie wasn't there, as she never is. Both
my father and Eddie have made their reappearances. They have hardly
changed at all. Of course, I must be careful when they come into the room.
Even deep in sleep I am aware that every move they make is tentative, as
if they sense they have been away. Yet, they do move and laugh and lend
those nights we meet a special radiance. Where is that girl who sat beside
me in that dingy classroom, filling it with spring?

Gone. Some things that go come round again. The crocus in the sun-
filled yard becomes the crocus in the shade, and sleeps, and is again warmed
by morning light. But some things that go are gone. Melzie died before I
found a way to attach any meaning to what we shared. Once we had danced
until we were the dance. For a moment that was enough, but the moment
disappeared. As a dilettante, I embraced the glitter, the pretty ever-chang-
ing surfaces, but I also longed for permanence. And it was a longing I was
consciously aware of, a longing that was articulated in much of what I read.

When Nicole said goodbye I hung up the phone and looked around.
The dust trapped in the light was only dust. No alligators hid beneath my
bed. My legs served well enough for walking but were not about to score
another touchdown. Everything was what it was, no more—constricted
to itself. I didn't even wonder if I'd miss the magic. I needed to grow up.

ACKNOWLEDGMENTS

I would like to thank my editor, Molly McGrath, for all she has done to make this a better book, and my wife Betsy for all she has done to make the last thirty years the better part of my life.

Made in the USA
San Bernardino, CA
11 November 2013